Renoir, detail; ***Two Sisters***

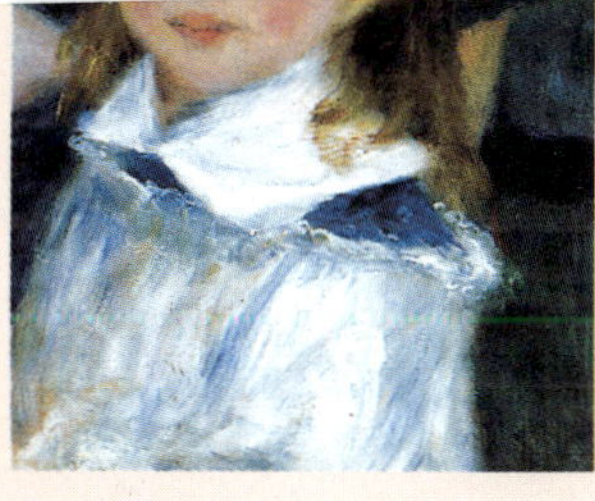

POST-IMPRESSIONISM IN CHICAGO

artistic story of the waning decades of the 1800s unfolds. Monet's pioneering Impressionist explorations reach an apex in his late series of *Stacks of Wheat*. Edgar Degas's *Ballet at the Paris Opéra* stands out among his luminous, asymmetrically composed paintings and pastels of dancers. They resonate with the work of the later artist Henri de Toulouse-Lautrec, whose arresting *At the Moulin Rouge* likewise captures the spectacle of Parisian nightlife. Georges Seurat's imposing *Sunday on La Grande Jatte—1884* reveals the artist's struggle with and ultimate transformation of Impressionism into something more structured and controlled. Vincent van Gogh and Paul Gauguin worked through Impressionism in their own ways, arriving, with *The Bedroom* and *Why Are You Angry?*, at unique expressions of their personal visions. Together, these masterpieces of Impressionist and Post-Impressionist art reveal the diverse approaches of gifted painters who redefined what it means to see and represent the world.

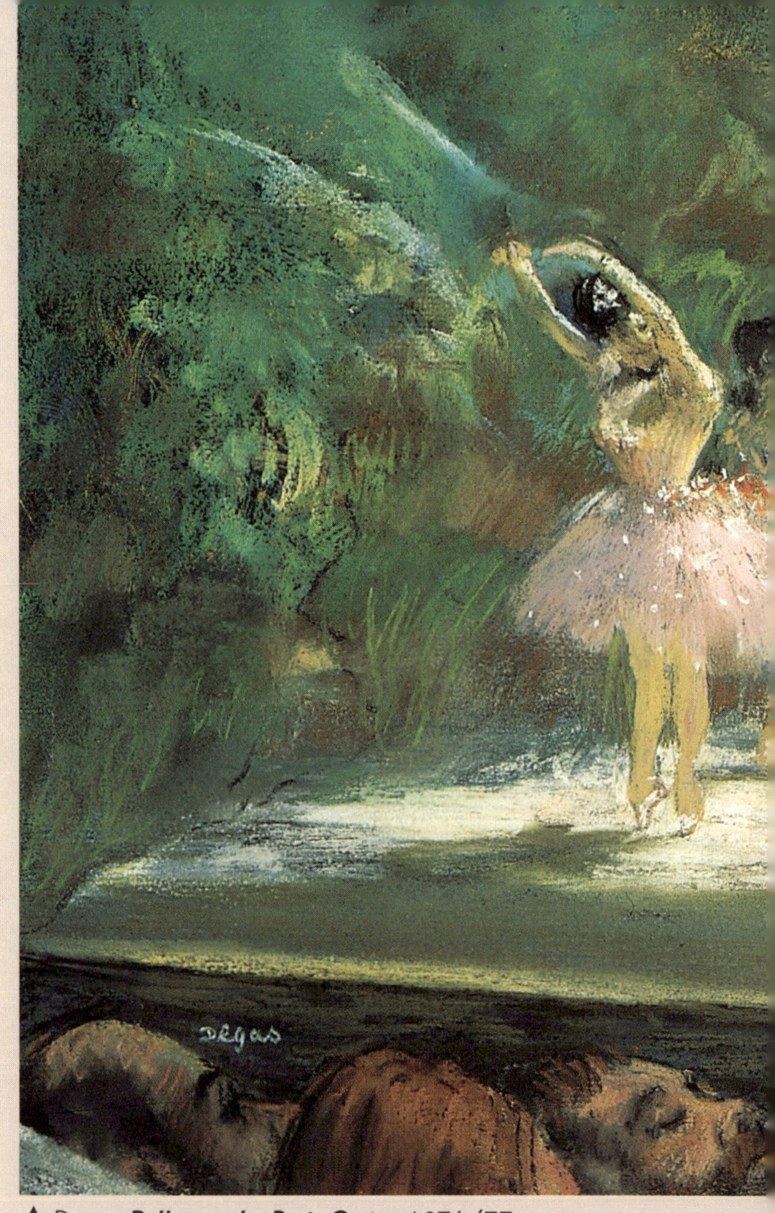

▲ Degas, ***Ballet at the Paris Opéra***, 1876/77

Approximately half of the work of **Edgar Degas** focuses on dancers—not only onstage but behind the scenes, at moments of rest or anticipation. In his ***Ballet at the Paris Opéra***, which was likely presented at the third Impressionist exhibition, in 1877, the iridescent setting glows with artificial light as ballerinas move across the stage.

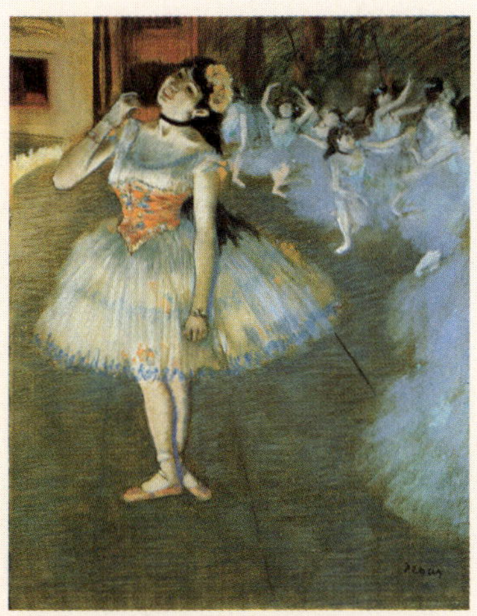

Degas, ***The Star***, c. 1880

In the foreground, male admirers and members of the orchestra turn their almost caricatural faces toward the stage for a glimpse of their favorite performers. The dark scrolls of two double basses looming prominently at the right seem to extend into the dancers' space and collapse the two realms. The radical cropping of figures and objects and the use of unusual or multiple perspectives to highlight surface appearance rather than spatial depth reflect the influence of Japanese woodblock prints.

Degas experimented with mixed-media techniques throughout his career. For ***Ballet at the Paris Opéra***, he first created a monotype—a unique print made by drawing and painting with black-brown ink on a metal plate and running it through a printing press—and then covered it with pastel. The dark monotype image, although obscured by the chalky pigment placed over it, gives the picture a shadowy, mysterious aura, while the pastel mimics the effects of artificial light and the textures of hair, skin, tulle, wood, and glitter.

Contents

Impressionism

The painters who would come to be known as the Impressionists were a disparate group united by their opposition to the traditional subjects and style promoted by fine-art académies and displayed at the state-sponsored, annual exhibitions, or Salons. Some artists abandoned large-scale, idealized history painting—which ranged from mythological and religious subjects to historical themes—and instead took up landscape, still life, portraits, and images of everyday life, genres that ranked low in traditional artistic hierarchy. In addition, rather than trying to meet conventional standards of even tonality and smooth finish, they used brighter colors and looser brushwork to reflect their direct observations of nature.

These avant-garde artists sought to capture the changing world around them in a new pictorial language, one that they could not learn in académies but had to invent on the spot and adjust to accommodate fleeting effects of weather, light, and movement. Their works reveal an interest in self-consciously modern themes: the spaces of the expanding, industrial city; the boundaries between public and private life in bourgeois society; and the relationship between nature and art.

The eight Impressionist group exhibitions held between 1874 and 1886 defined a new era in vanguard art and inspired the subsequent generation of painters.

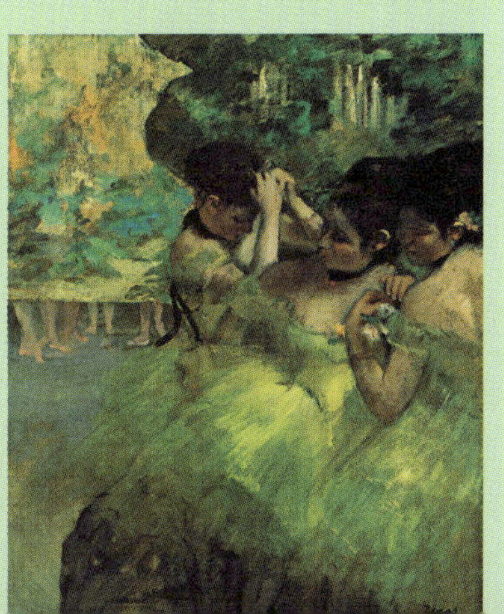

Edgar Degas (French, 1834–1917), **Yellow Dancers (In the Wings)**, 1874/76. Degas showed this work at the second Impressionist exhibition, in 1876.

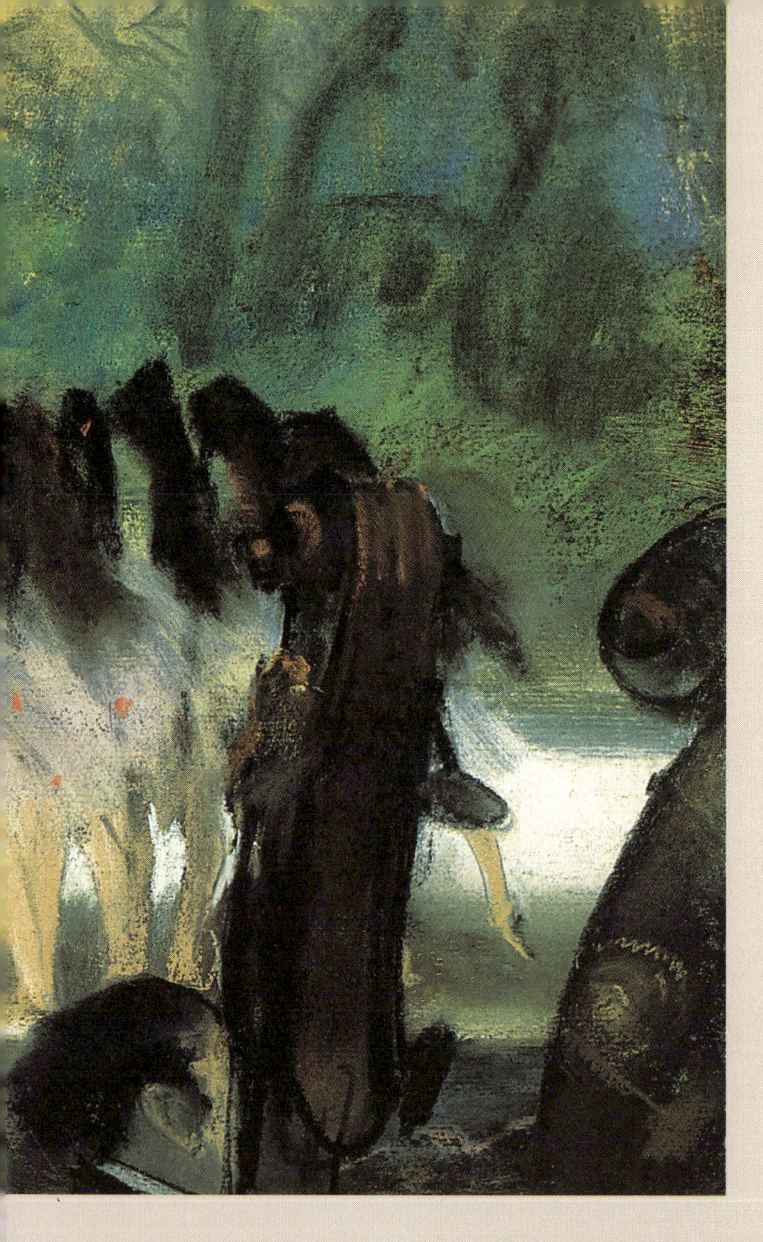

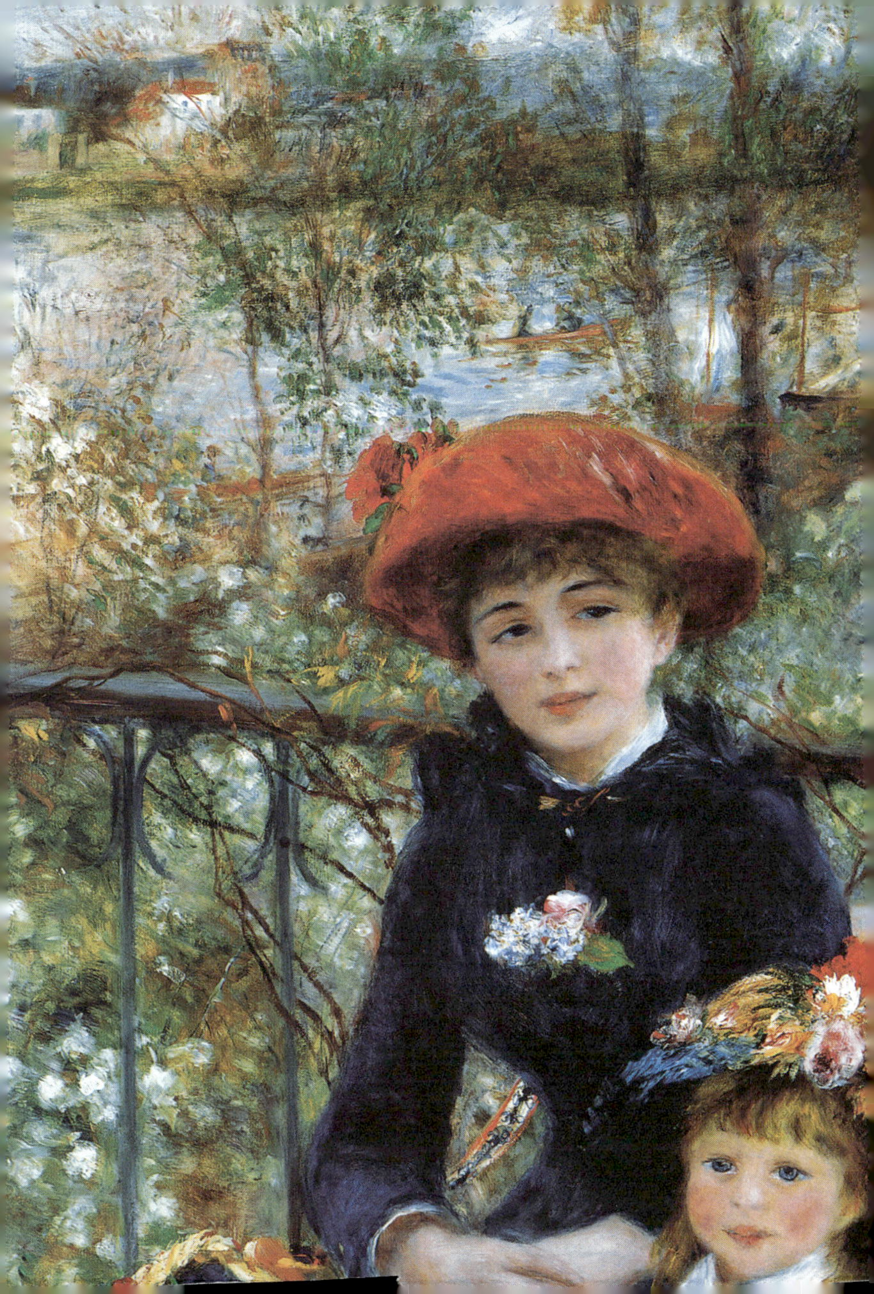

The lush, radiant paintings of **Pierre Auguste Renoir** are immediately recognizable. The rosy-cheeked children, graceful women, and elegant men of leisure who fill his canvases are rendered in meltingly soft hues and almost seem lit from within. His vivid works exalt earthly delights, burnishing them like cherished memories.

"For me," Renoir insisted, "a picture should be something likeable, joyous, and pretty—yes, pretty. There are enough ugly things in life for us not to add to them."

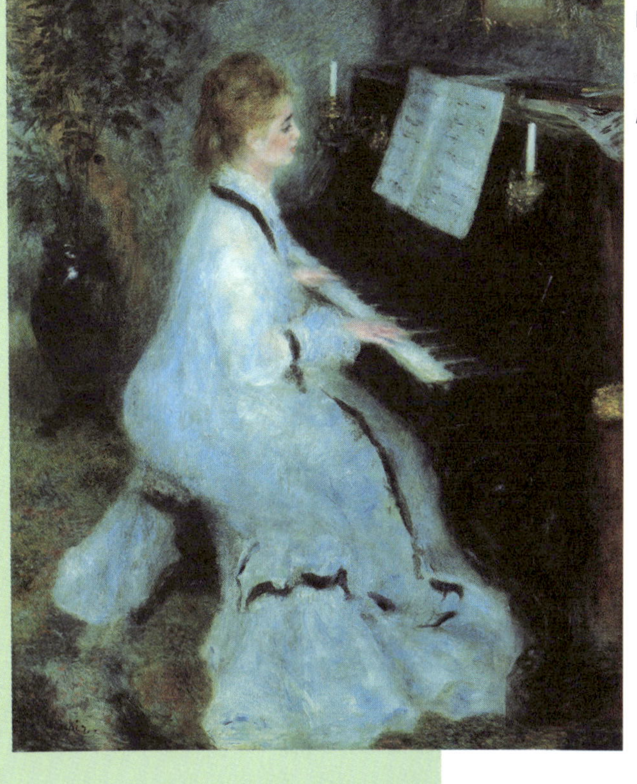

Pierre Auguste Renoir (French, 1841-1919), ***Woman at the Piano***, 1875/76

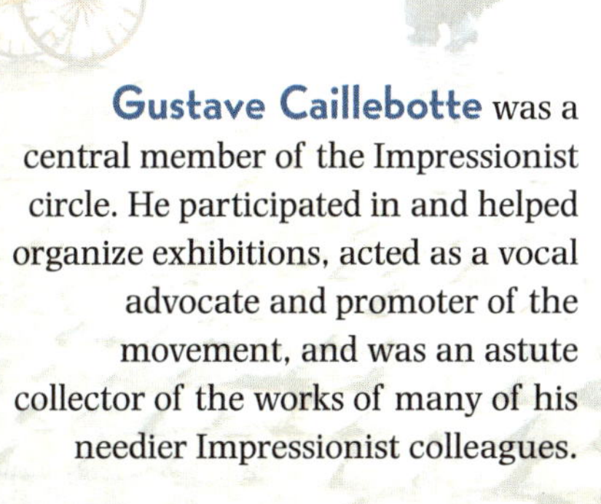

Gustave Caillebotte was a central member of the Impressionist circle. He participated in and helped organize exhibitions, acted as a vocal advocate and promoter of the movement, and was an astute collector of the works of many of his needier Impressionist colleagues.

After his death in 1894, a portion of the collection of important paintings he had amassed was given to the French nation, forming the core of the holdings of what is now the Musée d'Orsay in Paris.

Upon seeing ***Paris Street; Rainy Day*** at the third Impressionist exhibition in 1877, one critic proclaimed approvingly, "M. Caillebotte is an Impressionist in name only," regarding the large, polished canvas as superior to the "unfinished" works around it. Indeed, Caillebotte's solid, considered compositions seem more akin to academic paintings than to the quickly brushed, atmospheric productions of his colleagues. His working practice, too, was in stark contrast to *plein-air* painters who sought to capture the transient and the momentary.

Paris Street; Rainy Day is the culmination of numerous painted and drawn sketches in which Caillebotte toyed with details of costume, gesture, and facial expression for his figures, experimented with the placement of compositional elements, and sought to evoke the sweeping grandeur of Paris's newly paved boulevards and the soft gleam of slick cobblestones.

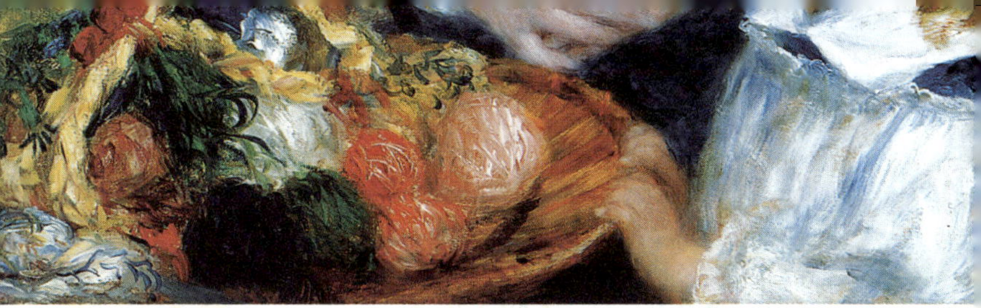

The setting, the terrace of the Restaurant Fournaise, is the same as Renoir's earlier *Rowers' Lunch* of 1875, but there is a palpable stylistic shift. In his earlier view of bourgeois leisure, softly brushed forms dissolve in the diffuse light that fills the canvas; here, the two girls have a greater solidity, and the landscape, while filled with exuberant foliage, includes trees whose vertical forms mirror the rigid wrought-iron bars of the railing. As always, Renoir transformed what he saw, infusing nature with the artifice necessary to create harmony.

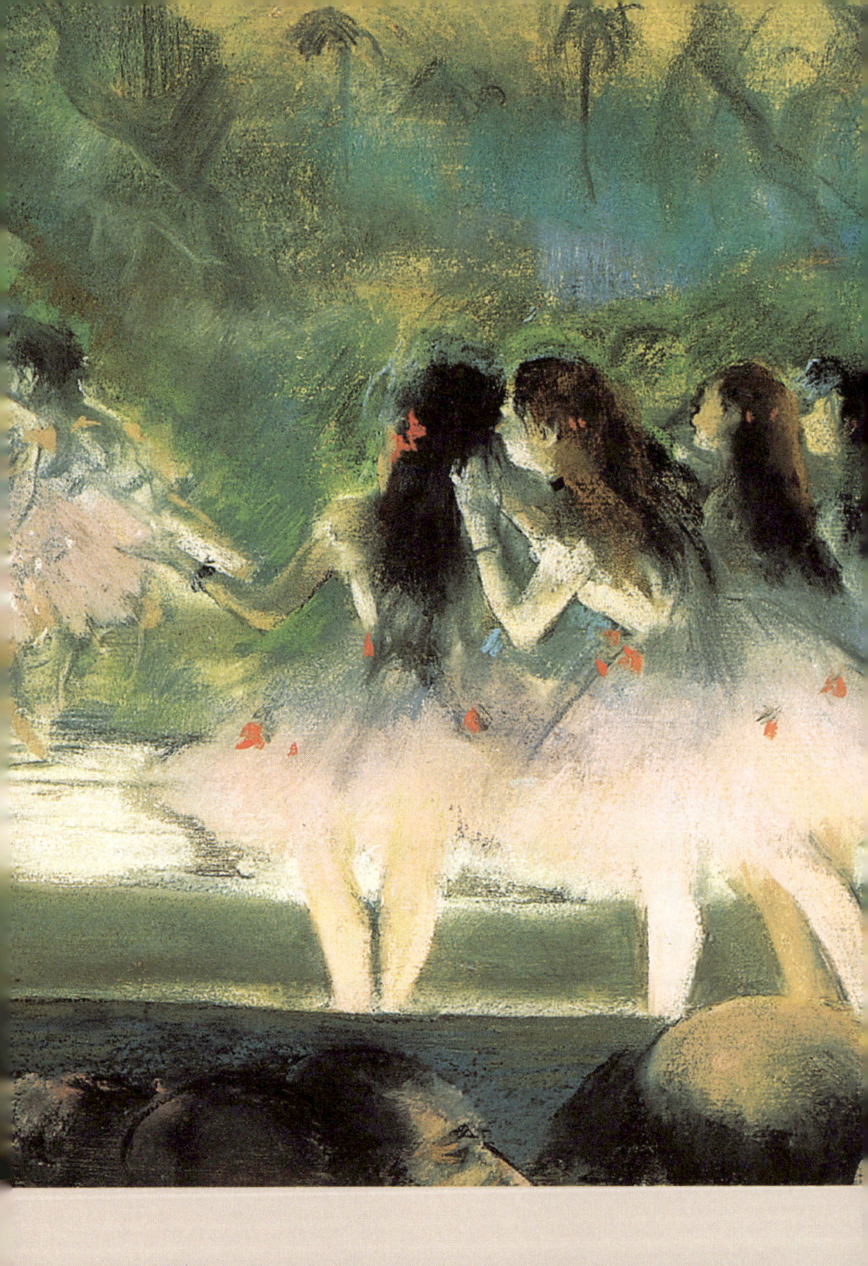

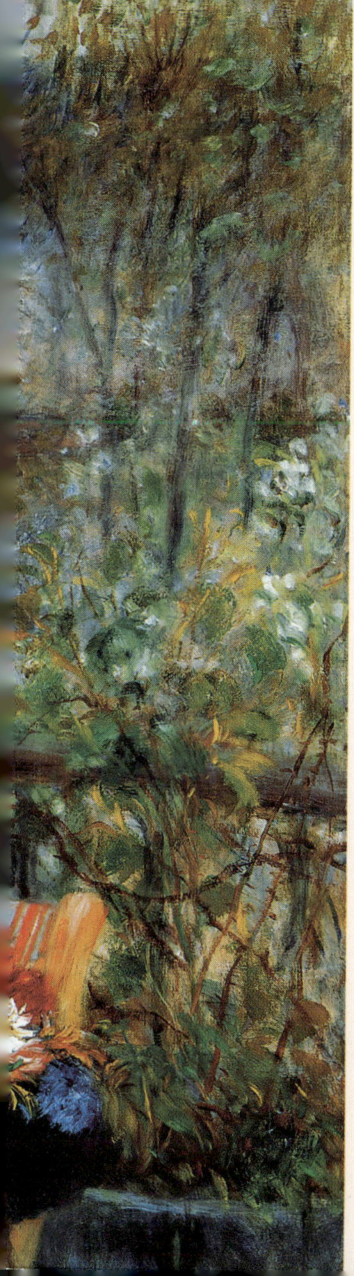

◀ Renoir, ***Two Sisters (On the Terrace)***, 1881

A celebration of the beauty of spring and the promise of youth, ***Two Sisters (On the Terrace)*** is a technical and compositional tour de force, a brilliant display of vibrant color and variegated brushwork. The nearly life-size figures occupy a shallow space in front of a railing; behind them quivers a lively, leafy landscape that brings their sharply delineated

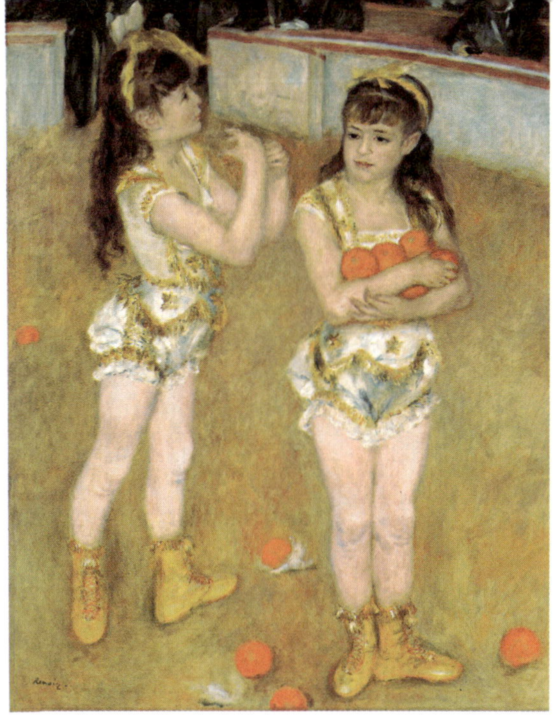

Renoir, ***Acrobats at the Cirque Fernando***, 1879

While he drew upon decidedly contemporary themes and images, his ultimate mission was to create a world of perfect peace and beauty and to provide respite from the trials of the everyday. His depictions of women in particular often seem less like portrayals of specific people than embodiments of the feminine ideal. Renoir's delight in his own craft is palpable in many of his works.

The lovely figure in his *Woman at the Piano*, for instance, seems almost to be an excuse for a virtuoso rendering of the play of light on soft fabric and gleaming metal, the delicate patterning of carpeting and plant leaves, and the subtle effects of color harmonies. Renoir refined his careful manipulation of pictorial elements to heighten the decorative impact of his works throughout his career.

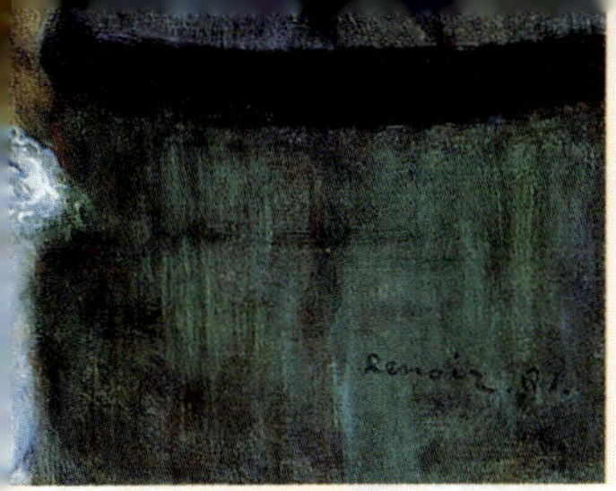

forms into vivid focus. The young child's irises are an almost startlingly clear, translucent blue, suggestive of the artist's desire to help us see the world afresh, through innocent eyes.

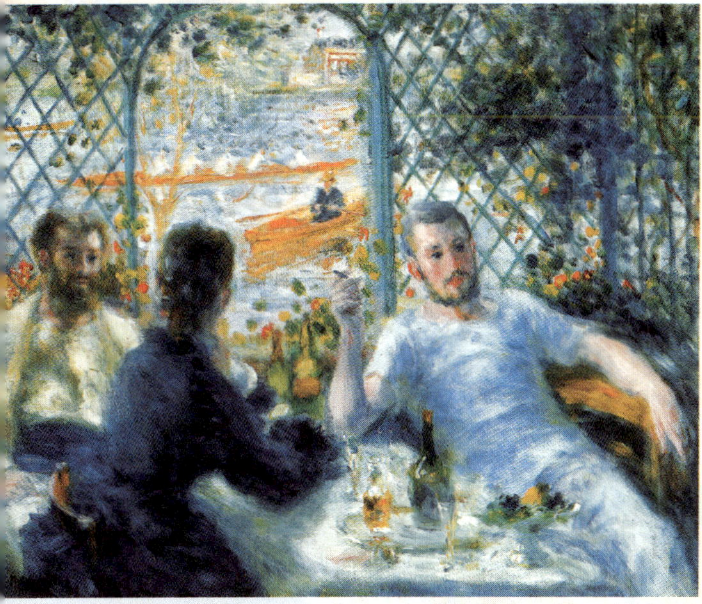

Renoir, ***Lunch at the Restaurant Fournaise (The Rowers' Lunch)***, 1875

Shown in 1882 at the seventh Impressionist exhibition, ***Two Sisters*** signaled Renoir's impending departure from Impressionism's preoccupation with rendering transient effects of light by means of flickering brushwork, while summarizing his dedication to the subjects and themes he had presented so buoyantly.

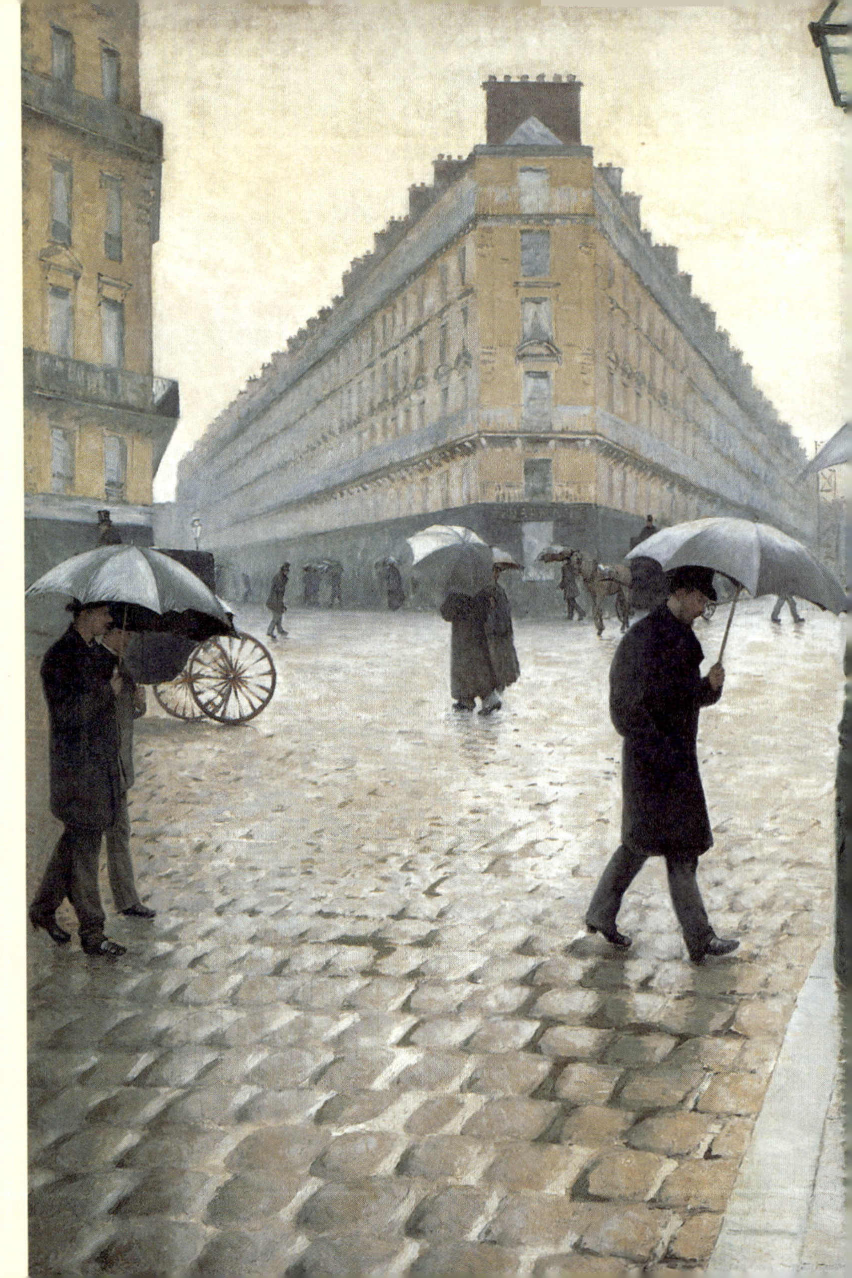

While he was an ardent supporter and patron of his colleagues Degas, Monet, and Renoir, his own art reveals a unique approach to the quintessential Impressionist subject of life in the city. His careful draftsmanship and precise handling, restrained palette, and use of monumental formats reflect his traditional art training. His asymmetrical compositions, cropping, and uncompromisingly modern subjects revealed a more radical sensibility.

Although his career was relatively brief and has often been regarded as uneven, Caillebotte created a number of iconic images that can be ranked among the masterpieces of the Impressionist era, including his most famous painting, ***Paris Street; Rainy Day***.

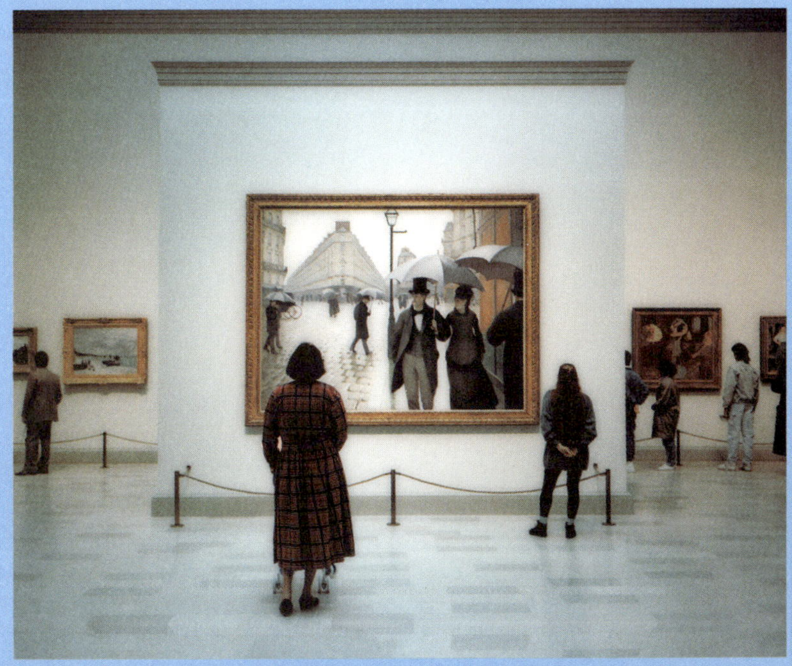

Thomas Struth (German, born 1954), ***Art Institute 2***, 1990

Caillebotte shared with the Impressionists an interest in the strikingly modern spaces of Paris and the people who populated them, but rather than attempting to capture a slice of contemporary life, he manipulated these themes in the interest of larger formal concerns.

In this work, Caillebotte combined apparent spontaneity with precise choreography; the glances, postures, and relative sizes of the well-dressed couples and individuals who pepper the composition all complement and reinforce the converging diagonals that dictate the painting's perspective.

Gustave Caillebotte (French, 1848–1894), ***Paris Street; Rainy Day***, 1877

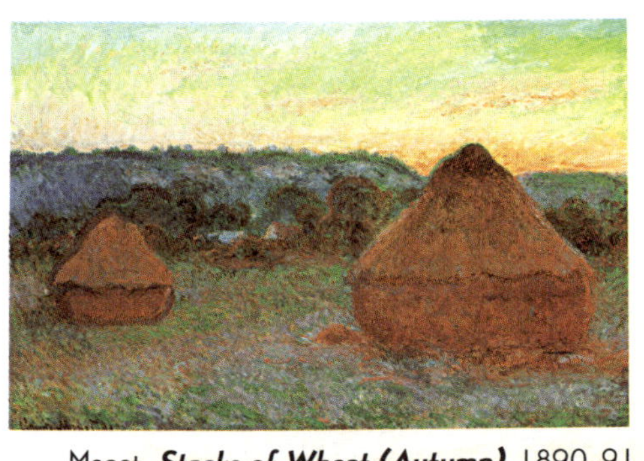

Monet, ***Stacks of Wheat (Autumn)***, 1890–91

In his series of stacks of wheat, Monet challenged himself to find and capture the variety of pictorial interest and sense of monumentality one can encounter in even the humblest of subjects. The fifteen- to twenty-foot-high wheat stacks, built by farmers after reaping the harvest, are only the titular subjects of his exploration; the true protagonists are atmosphere and light—harshly slanting or diffuse, sparkling or muted, rich and golden or brittle and blue.

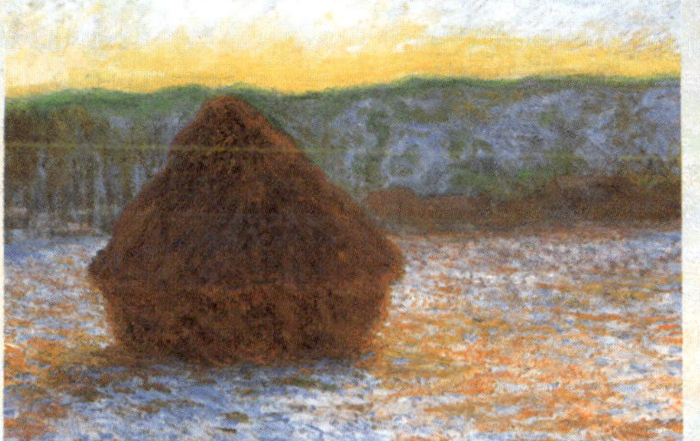

Monet, ***Stack of Wheat (Thaw, Sunset)***, 1890–91

His ***Stacks of Wheat (End of Summer)*** perfectly evokes the effect of light on a drowsy, late-summer afternoon. The warm sun delicately dapples the background foliage and picks out strands of wheat on the right side of the stacks.

Claude Monet is perhaps the artist most closely associated with Impressionism. It was after all his seascape *Impression—Sunrise* (1872–73; Paris, Musée Marmotton-Monet), shown at the first Impressionist exhibition, in 1874, that gave the movement its name.

Arrival of the Normandy Train, Gare Saint-Lazare, reveals the artist's preoccupation with contemporary life and demonstrates his ability to evoke the subtle, ever-changing effects of dissipating steam and swirls of smoke.

For me, a landscape har
but it lives by virtue of

Monet was deeply interested in rendering instantaneously what he saw in the world before him, but he recognized that the constant alteration of nature itself made this nearly impossible. He envisioned a series of works representing a particular scene at different times of the day, hoping to suggest in a number of discrete moments the effect of the whole. One of these is a large group of images depicting the stacks of wheat in the fields around his home in Giverny.

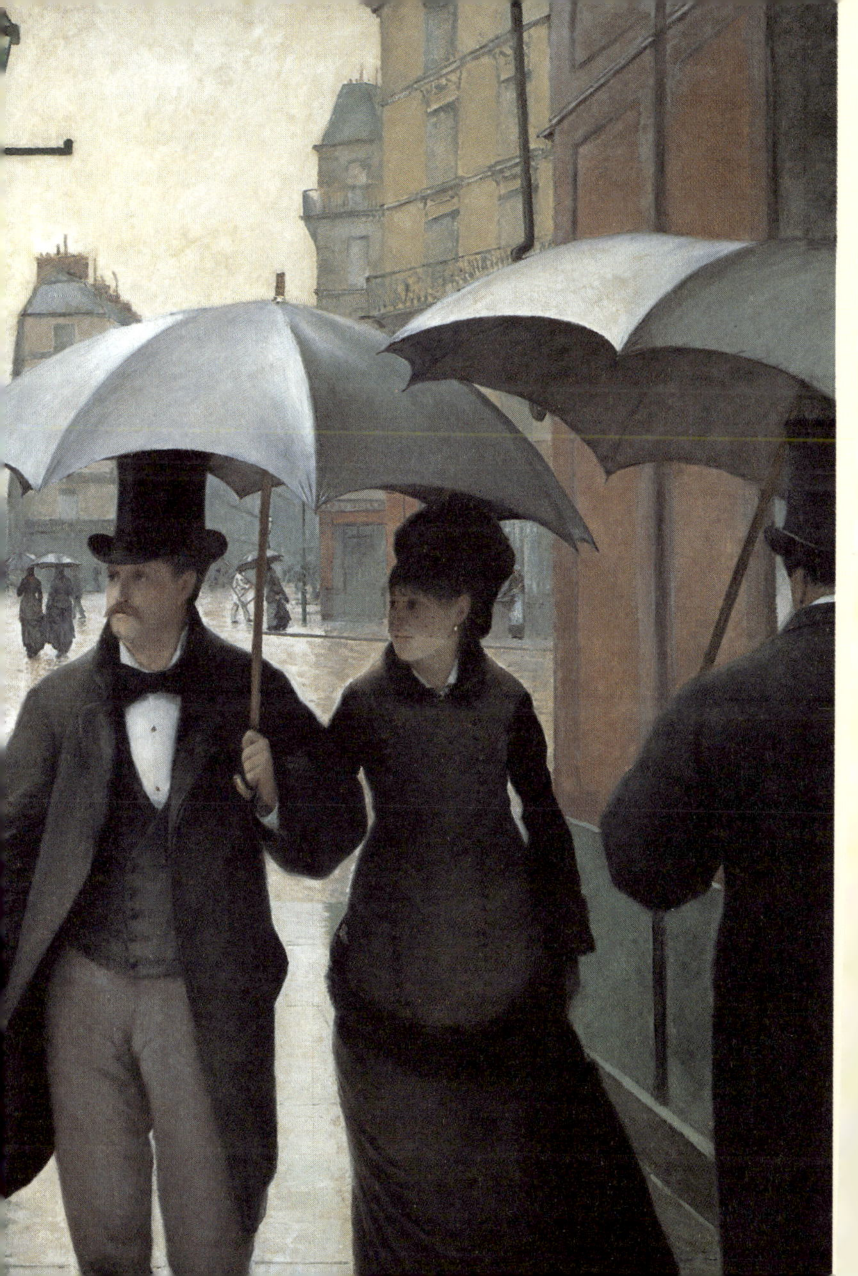

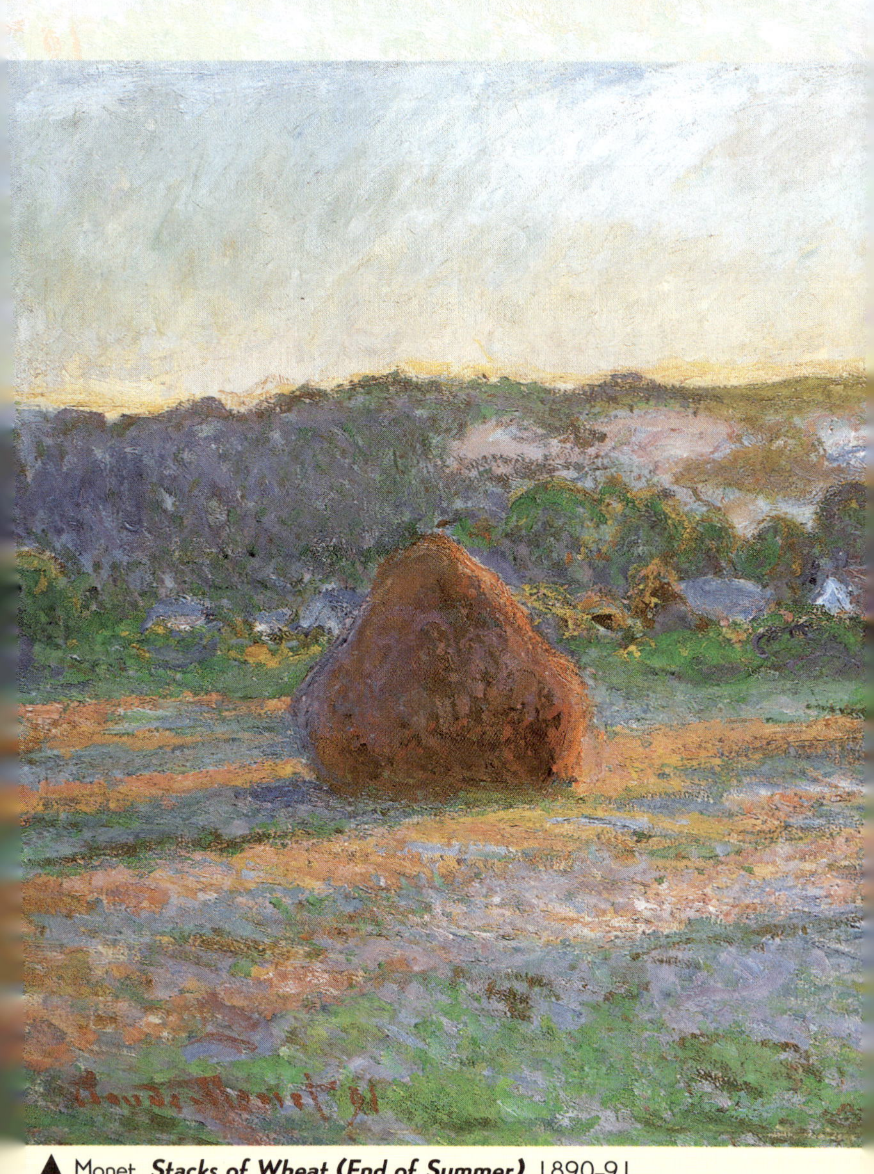

▲ Monet, ***Stacks of Wheat (End of Summer)***, 1890–91

Georges Seurat (French, 1859–1891), ***Seated Woman with a Parasol***, 1884/85. This is one of twenty-eight drawings Seurat created as studies for ***La Grande Jatte***. He also produced thirty-one painted sketches.

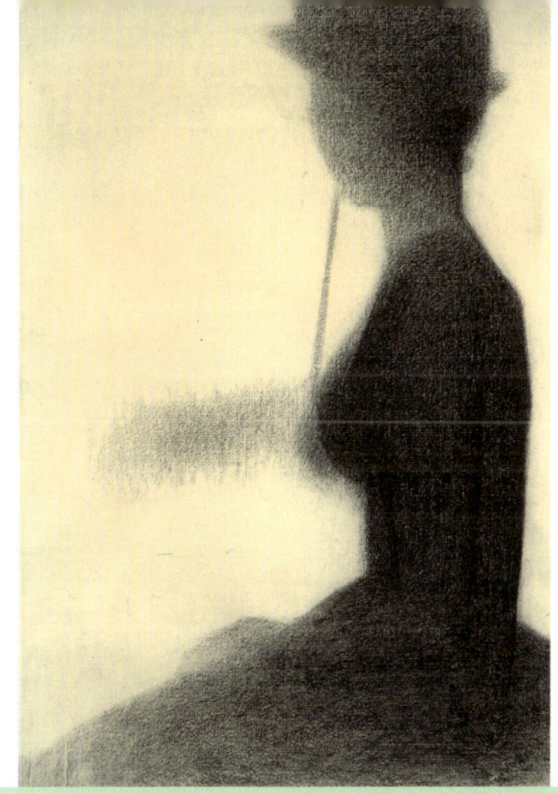

Georges Seurat was as concerned as Monet with the ability or inability of art to capture the ever-changing world. Seurat's early works, with their light palettes and lively brushwork, show his debt to the Impressionists, but as his art matured, he was increasingly interested in creating something less ephemeral and more permanent. He came to consider the vibrant and spontaneous paintings he did in nature as sketches for larger compositions rather than as finished works.

Like Caillebotte, Seurat had an academic training, which can be seen in his extensive use of painted and drawn studies in developing his paintings. His method reached its apex in his masterpiece, ***A Sunday on La Grande Jatte—1884***, on which he labored for two years, from 1884 to 1886. The subject of this monumental

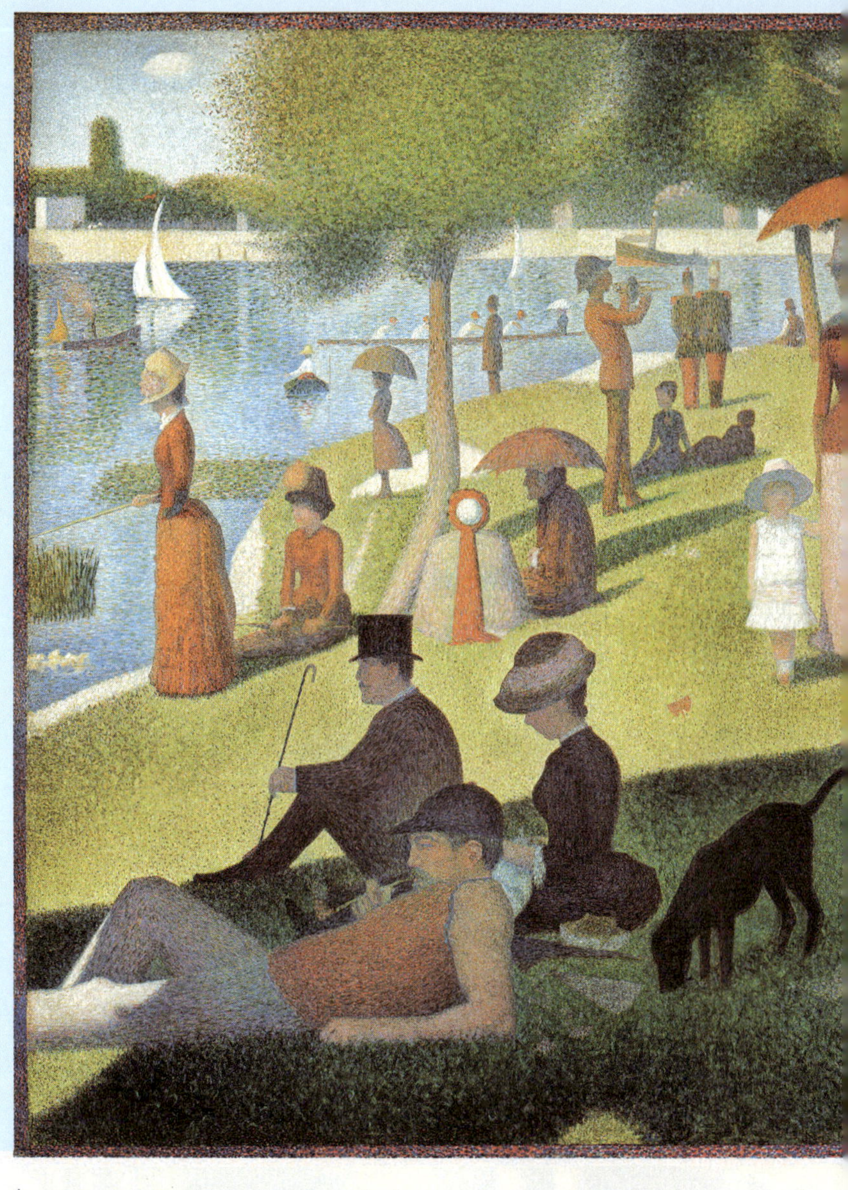

▲ Seurat, ***A Sunday on La Grande Jatte—1884***, 1884–86

In 1890 Seurat summarized the aesthetic that motivated his work: "Art is Harmony. Harmony is the analogy of opposites, the analogy of similarities of tone, of tint, of line." This creation of harmony and balance out of disparate elements is evident everywhere in ***La Grande Jatte***. Each of the nearly fifty figures who populate Seurat's island park seems fixed in time and space and in relation to each other. They are exactly where they should be; one can scarcely imagine them anywhere else.

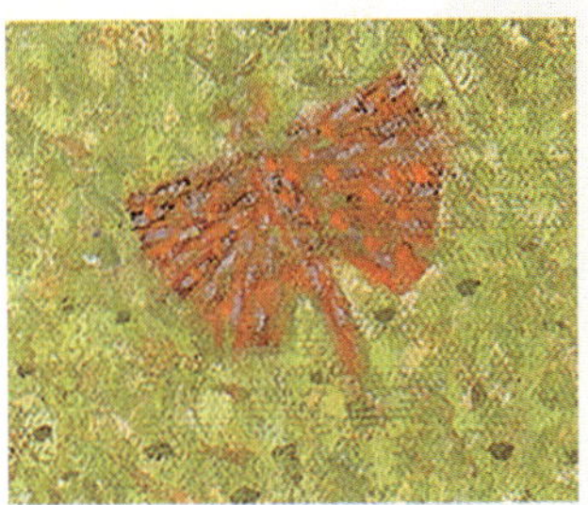

Seurat, detail; ***La Grande Jatte,*** 1884–86

Seurat transformed the free, sketchy brushwork of the Impressionists into a more regular screen of dots, dashes, and lines of discrete touches of paint—a style that would come to be known as pointillism. He developed this technique in order to exploit the way the human eye perceives color and heighten the luminosity of his painting. Drawing on current optical theory, Seurat believed that any color is heightened when placed beside its "complement." When the complements red and green are put side by side, for instance, the red will seem redder and the green, greener. Throughout ***La Grande Jatte***, one finds, for instance, touches of green in the dark folds of red dresses and spots of blue shadow on yellow straw hats. Seurat was also aware of how the optical mixture of colors in the eye is different from combining them on the palette. Juxtaposing related shades on a canvas (yellows and greens, for example) will create a more vivid and luminous effect than if the colors are mixed before being applied.

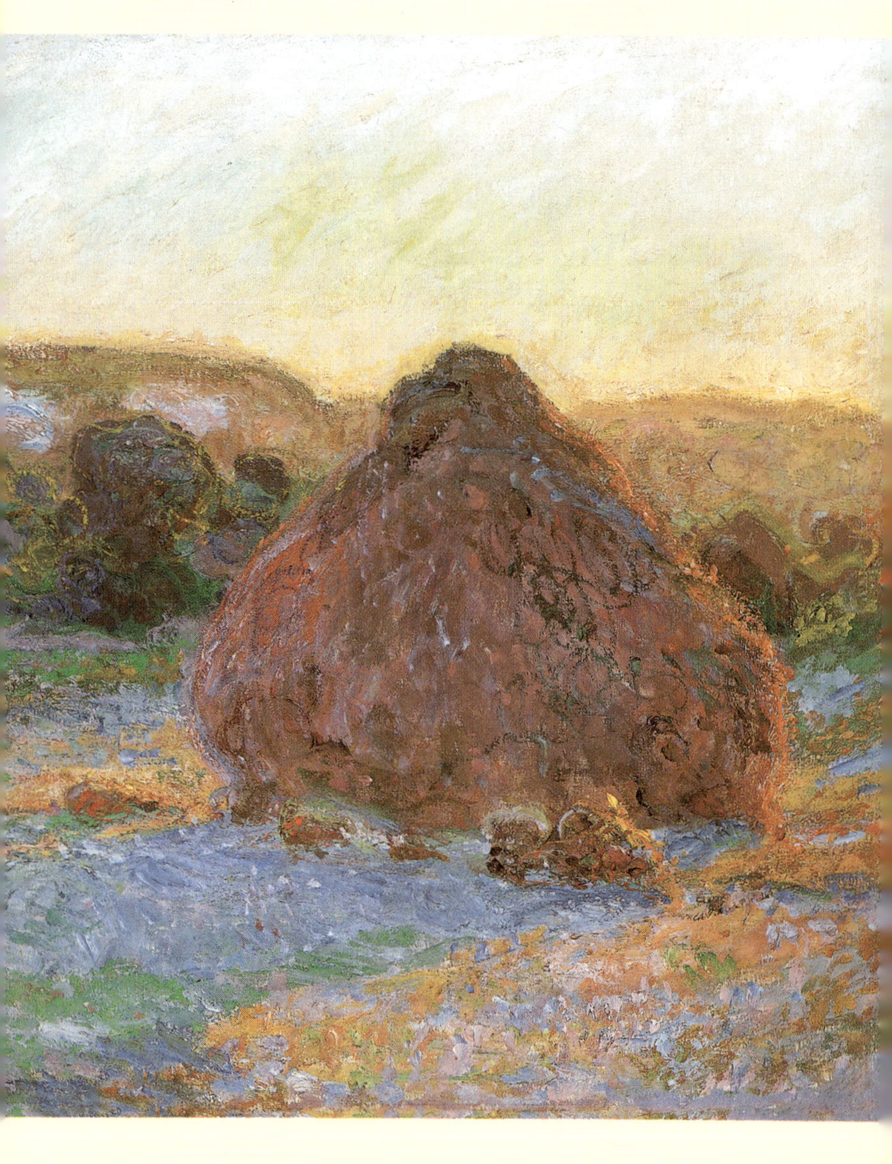

In other works, the earthy dampness of wheat beneath thawing snow is almost palpable. Monet exhibited fifteen of his *Stacks of Wheat* paintings together in 1891 at the Galerie Durand-Ruel in Paris. He believed the cumulative effect of the series was the key to representing the endless variety of nature. The Art Institute is therefore fortunate to house six *Stacks of Wheat*, three of them from the 1891 show.

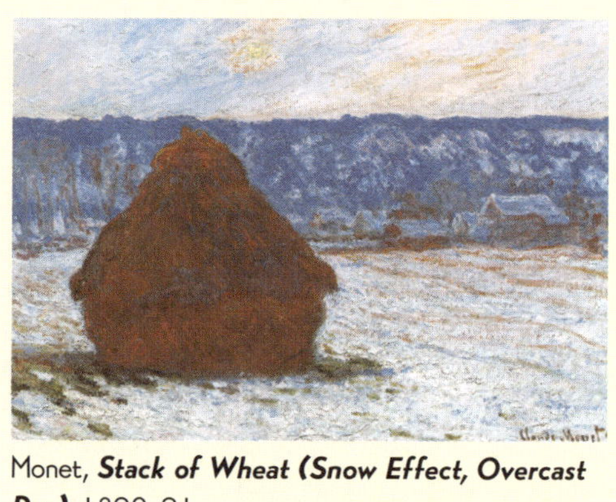

Monet, ***Stack of Wheat (Snow Effect, Overcast Day)***, 1890–91

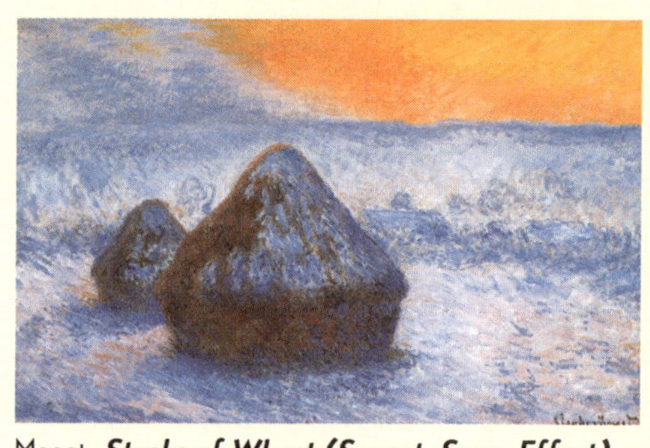

Monet, ***Stacks of Wheat (Sunset, Snow Effect)***, 1890–91

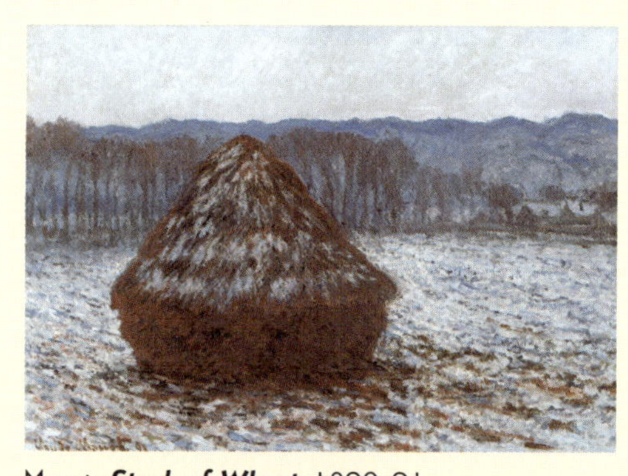

Monet, ***Stack of Wheat***, 1890–91

exists at all as a landscape, because its appearance is constantly changing; surroundings—the air and light—which vary continually. Claude Monet

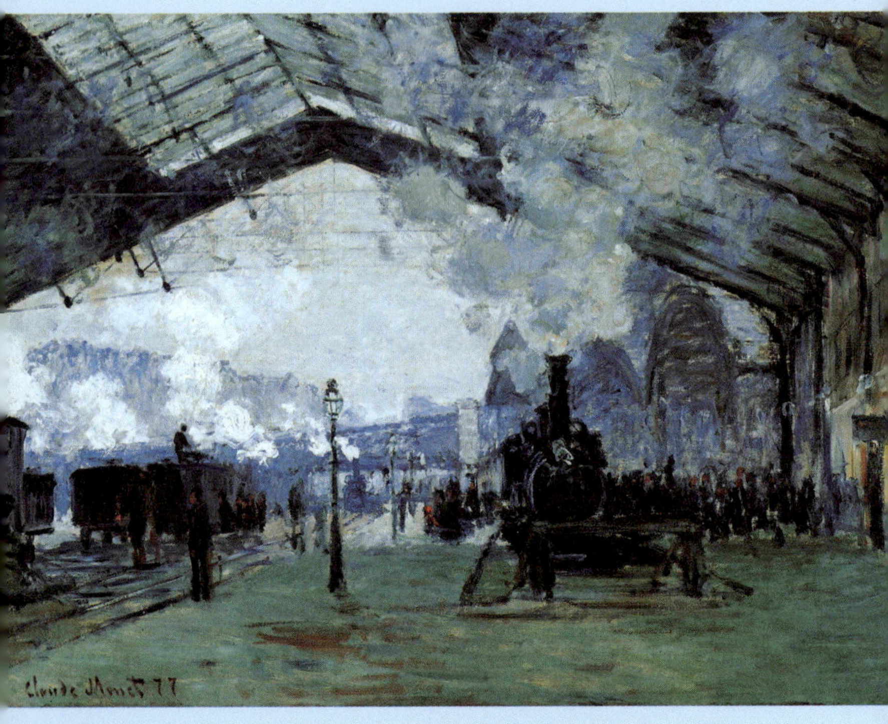

Claude Monet (French, 1840–1926), ***Arrival of the Normandy Train, Gare Saint-Lazare***, 1877. Monet exhibited seven paintings of the Saint-Lazare train station in 1877. It was his first series to explore a single subject at different times and in different light conditions.

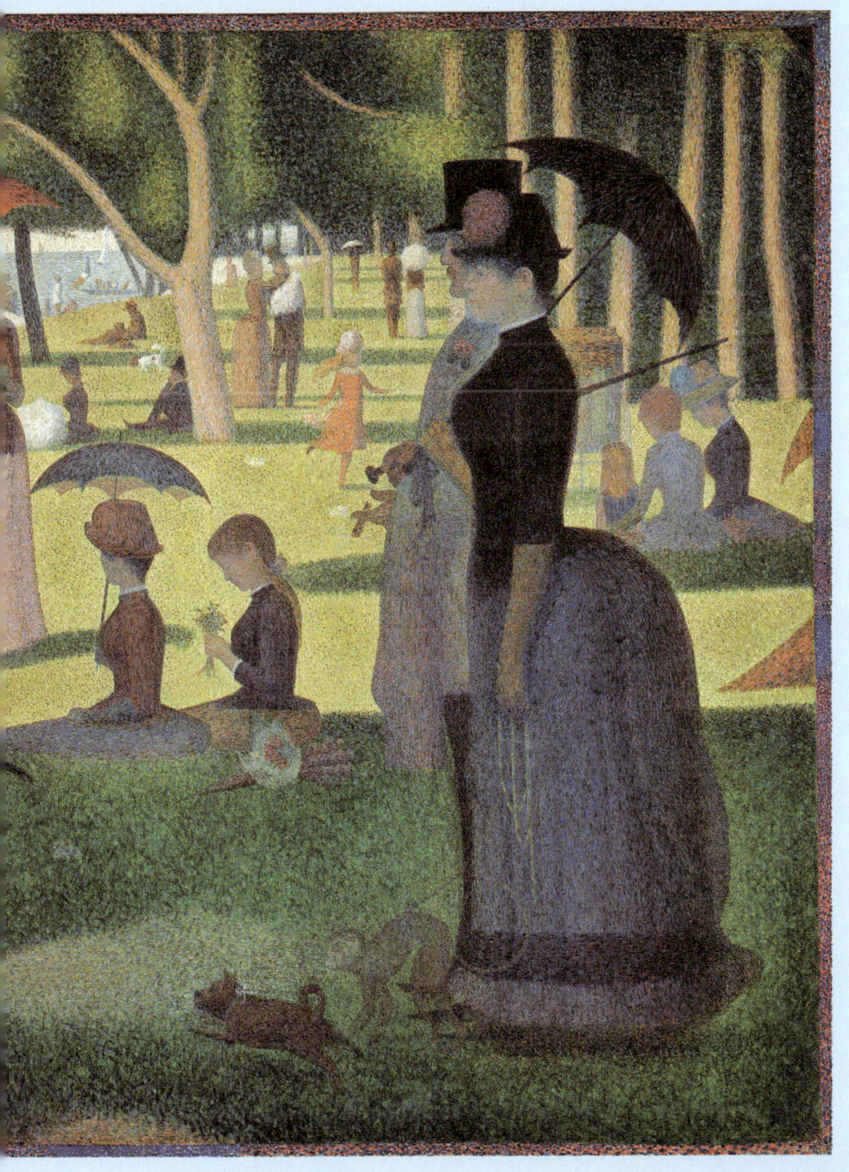

Seurat, ***Trees***, 1884. This large drawing is an early study of the landscape setting.

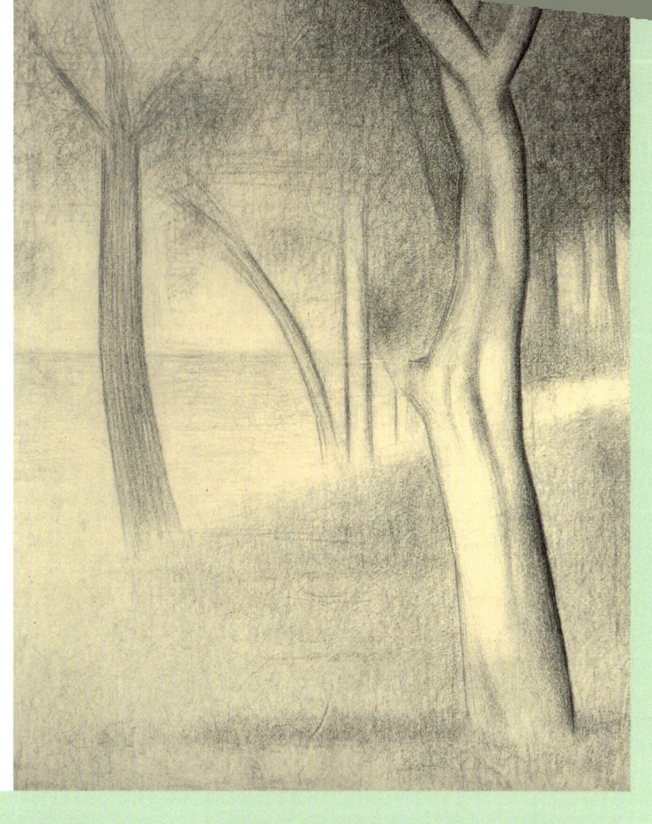

work—contemporary Parisians enjoying a day of leisure in a riverside park—is clearly rooted in Impressionism, but the approach marks a new direction. The rigidity and solidity of the figures and the deliberate compositional rhythms contribute to a feeling of stasis and timelessness.

As Seurat wrote in 1888, "I want to make modern people, in their essential traits, move about as they do on those [Greek] friezes, and place them on canvases organized by harmonies of color, by direction of the tones in harmony with the lines, and by the directions of those lines." He exhibited the large painting at the eighth, and final, Impressionist exhibition, in 1886, inaugurating a new movement in art that would be called Neo-Impressionism.

Vincent van Gogh (Dutch, 1853–1890), ***Self-Portrait***, 1886/87

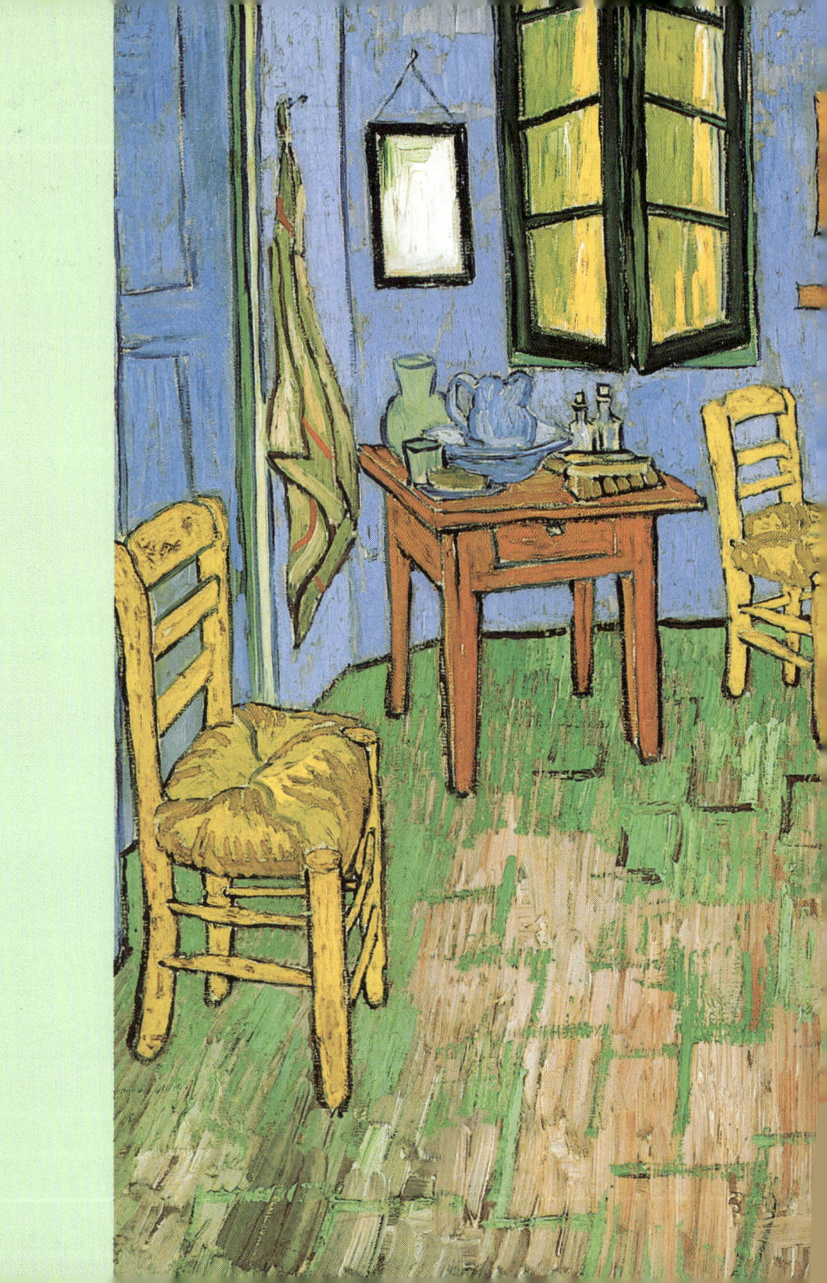

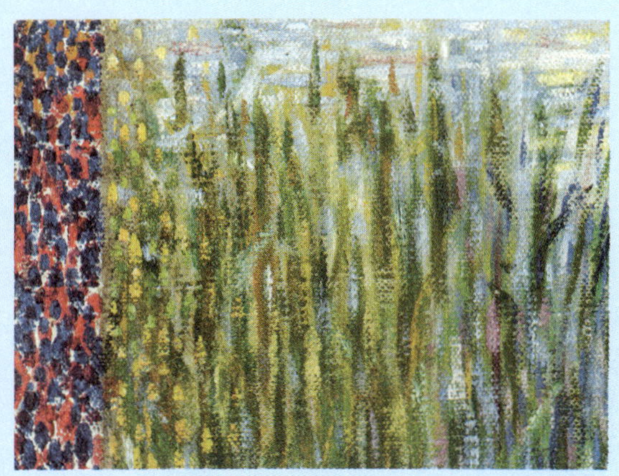

Seurat, detail; ***La Grande Jatte***, 1884–86. Around 1888/89, the artist added a painted border of complementary dots all around the canvas, a further extension of his experiments with color.

Other artists would experiment with Seurat's pointillist style, but the movement would be short-lived. More enduring were the new elements—simplification of form, a classical mode of spatial organization, and a sophisticated sense of decorative unity—that Seurat introduced into avant-garde art.

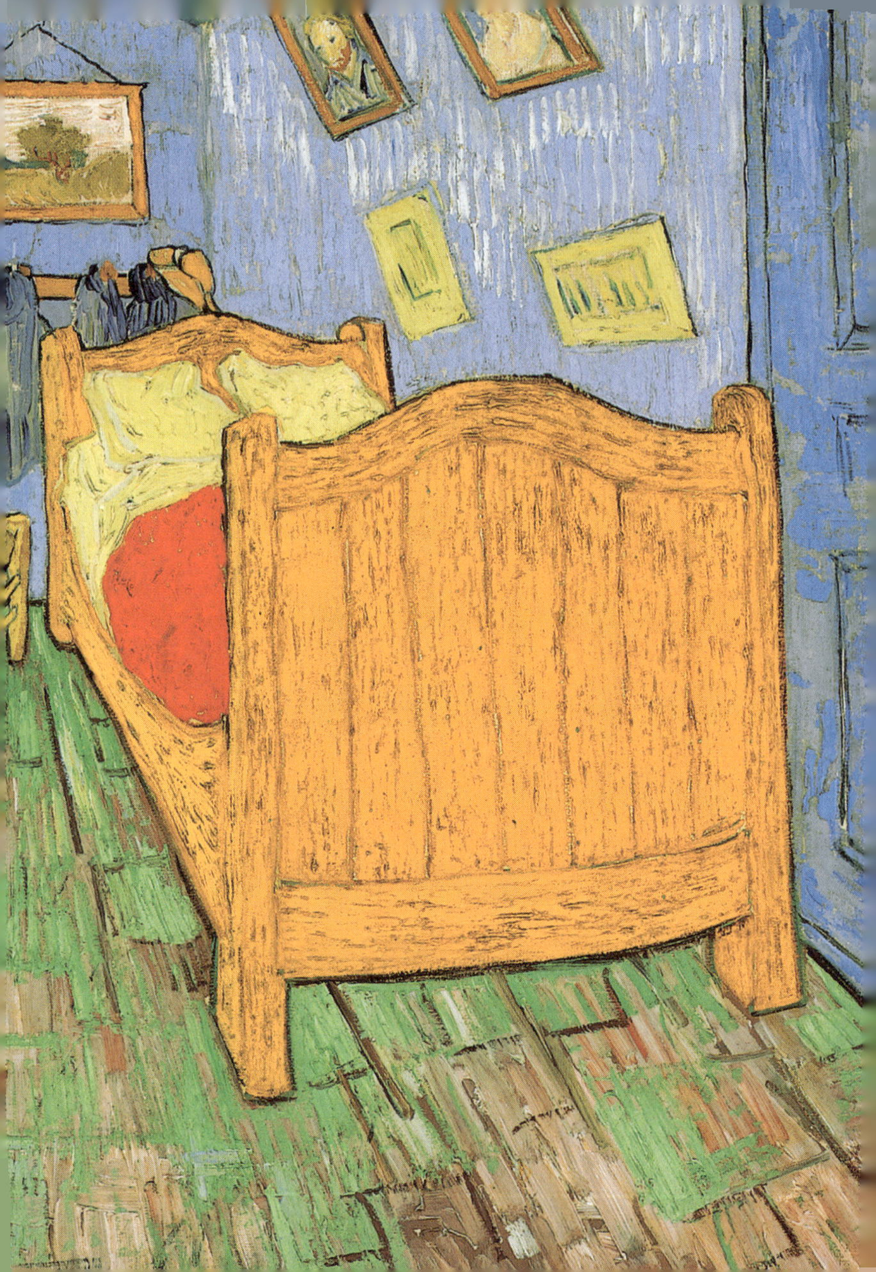

Although **Vincent van Gogh** had visited Paris a number of times in the 1870s, his first exposure to the Impressionists seems to have been in 1886. It is unclear whether he attended the eighth Impressionist exhibition, but the latest artistic developments in the capital undoubtedly influenced his work. He lightened his palette, which had previously been dominated by earth tones, and sought to replicate the Impressionists' flickering brushwork.

His *Self-Portrait* of 1886/87 reflects his experimentation with Neo-Impressionism; the background—filled with discrete touches of complementary greens and reds—reveals his absorption of contemporary color theory. Van Gogh would soon abandon pointillist handling, but Seurat's poetic notion of a "harmony of contrasts" would continue to haunt him. He left Paris in 1888, resettling in Arles, in the south of France, where he dreamed of setting up a "Studio of the South"—a cooperative of like-minded artists that he hoped would be led by Paul Gauguin, whom he had met the previous November.

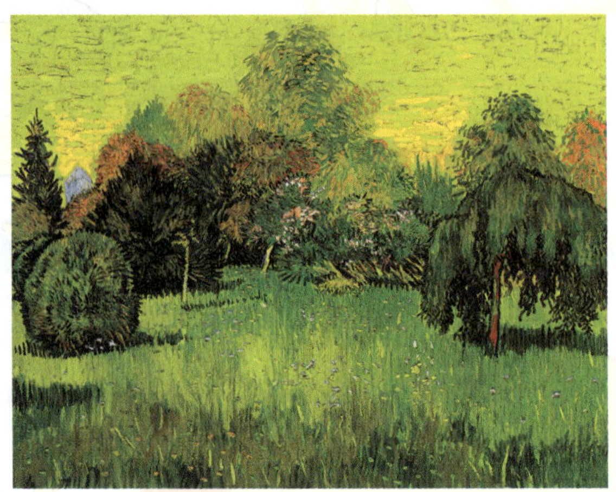

Van Gogh, ***The Poet's Garden***, 1888. This small park was just across the square from Van Gogh's studio in Arles.

In ***The Bedroom***, Van Gogh wished to express an "absolute restfulness." Apparently, he thought that the inclusion of all six complementary colors would result in chromatic equilibrium, thus communicating calm. However, to our eyes, the palette of orange, aquamarine, lime green, blood red, and chrome yellow seems to throb with intensity. This nervous energy is heightened by the floor, which appears to plunge precipitously, thrusting the foot of the bed toward the viewer. Van Gogh painted three versions of the subject; the Art Institute example dates from 1889, indicating that the motif remained profoundly significant for him even after Gauguin had come and gone and Van Gogh's attempt at an artistic brotherhood had failed.

Perhaps no artist captured the spectacular nocturnal life of Paris at the end of the nineteenth century more memorably than **Henri de Toulouse-Lautrec**. His paintings, drawings, and, particularly, posters define the vibrancy, along with the melancholy, of Montmartre and the larger-than-life personalities who thrived there.

He pursued traditional art studies for several years, but it was Edgar Degas who would prove to be his most lasting influence. Lautrec's skewed perspective, cropped figures, and intense attention to physiognomy bordering on caricature all have resonance with the oeuvre of the older artist.

Lautrec marked new artistic territory for himself in 1891, when his large color lithographic poster *Moulin Rouge, La Goulue* appeared on the walls of Paris.

The Moulin Rouge attracted an adventurous, middle-class clientele, as well as members of the avant-garde, all of whom relished its provocative performances and intoxicating sexual energy. The dance hall was an enduring source of inspiration for the artist; in his portrayals of its habitués and performers, whom he knew intimately, he experimented with bold formal innovations, a variety of different media, and themes of celebrity, the allure of the modern city, and the isolation one finds even in a crowd.

Henri de Toulouse-Lautrec (French, 1864–1901),
Moulin Rouge, La Goulue, 1891

At the Moulin Rouge is perhaps one of Lautrec's most ambitious compositions. The sharply angled banister that cuts a diagonal swath along the bottom left and the green, dimly reflecting mirrors in the background enclose the vertiginous space of the balcony overlooking the dance floor of the cabaret. Depicted are regular denizens of the Moulin Rouge—including Jane Avril, a red-headed dancer who was a perennial Lautrec subject. In the right background, we see the infamous La Goulue (the star

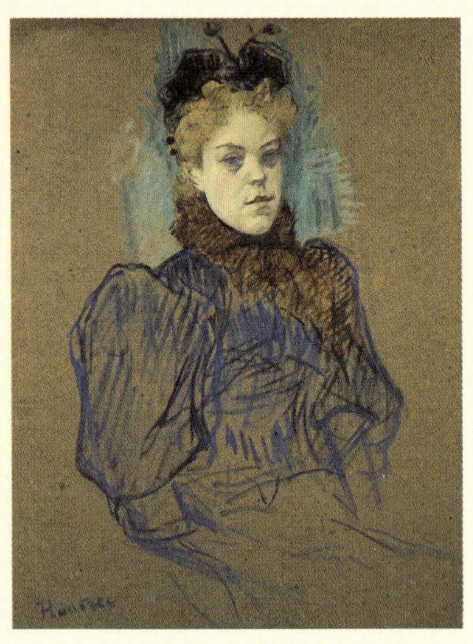

Lautrec, ***May Milton***, 1895

▼ Lautrec, ***At the Moulin Rouge***, 1892/95

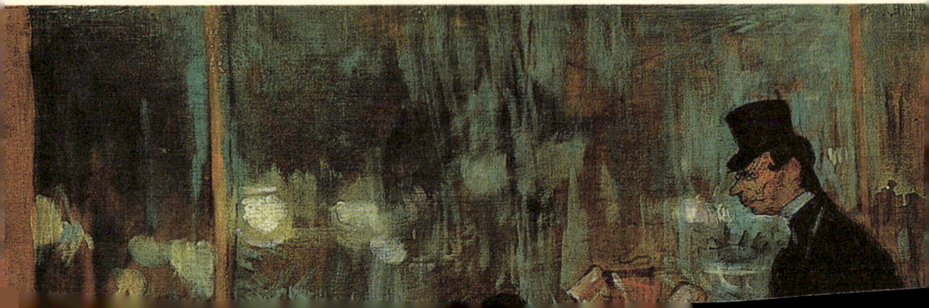

In anticipation of Gauguin's arrival, Van Gogh produced a number of "decorations" to adorn the Yellow House, the name he gave his home and studio; these include images of his now-famous sunflowers, portraits of his friends, garden scenes, and a view of his own bedroom. His modest subjects reflect themes of his everyday life, but he imbued them with symbolic and expressive qualities that transcend the quotidian. As he wrote to his brother Theo in October 1888, "Instead of trying to reproduce exactly what I see before me, I make more arbitrary use of color to express myself more forcefully."

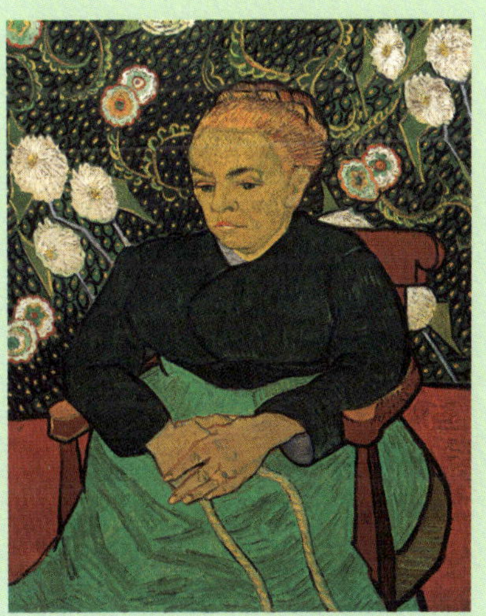

Van Gogh, ***Madame Roulin Rocking the Cradle (La Berceuse)***, 1889. This painting, showing the wife of the local postman, is also a repetition of a composition Van Gogh initially created to decorate the Yellow House.

◀ Van Gogh, ***The Bedroom***, 1889. The original version of this subject is in the Van Gogh Museum, Amsterdam.

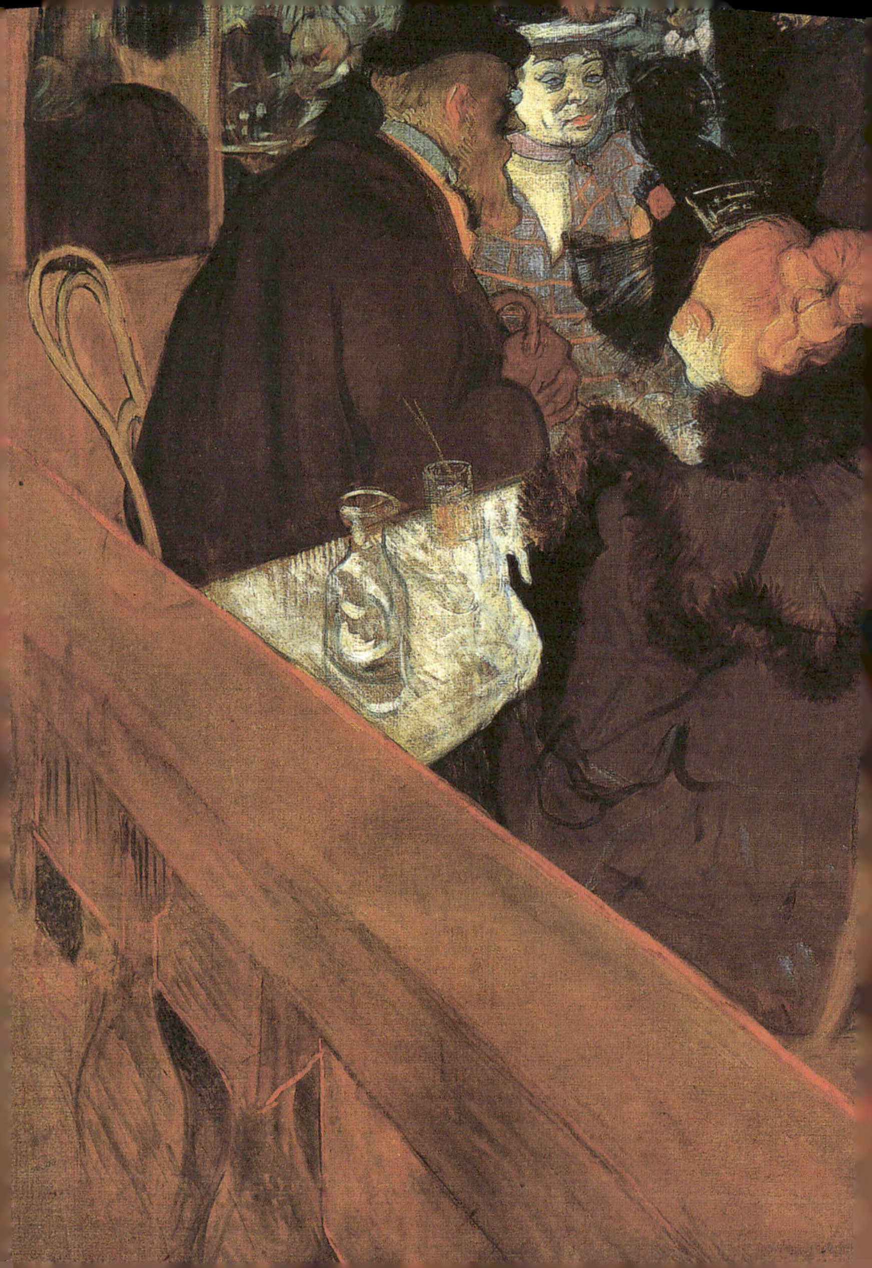

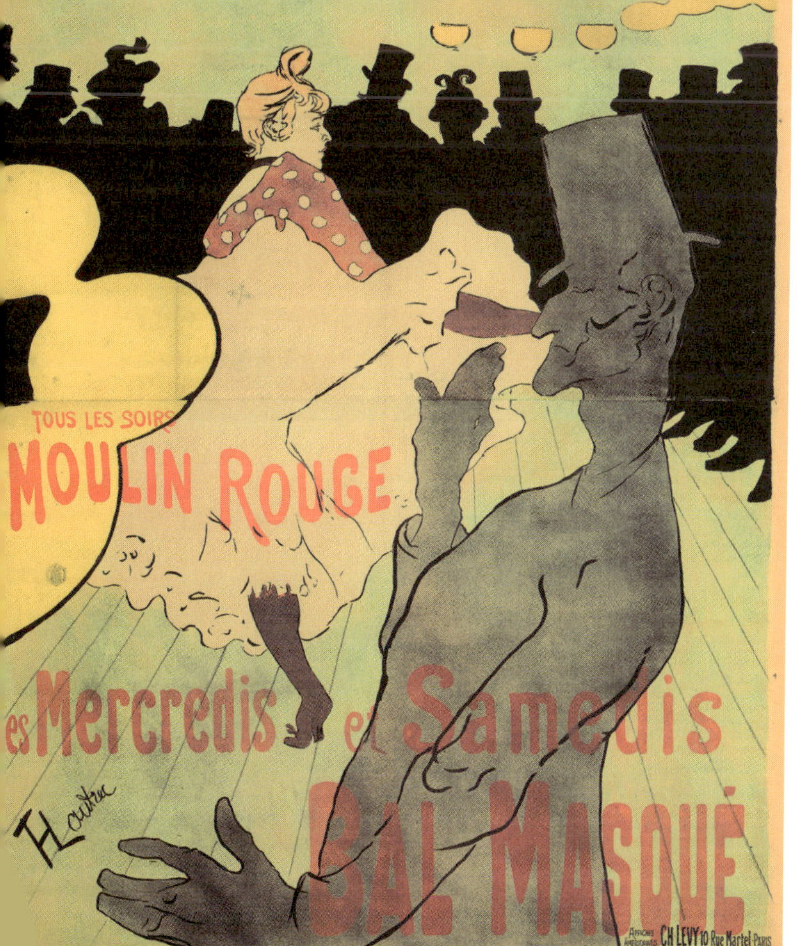
MOULIN ROUGE
MOULIN ROUGE
MOULIN ROUGE
CONCERT
BAL
TOUS Les SOIRS
LA GOULUE
TOUS LES SOIRS
MOULIN ROUGE
es Mercredis et Samedis
BAL MASQUÉ
AFFICHES AMÉRICAINES CH. LEVY 10 Rue Martel PARIS

of the artist's breakthrough poster) adjusting her hair while her sister looks on. The diminutive Lautrec and his lanky cousin Gabriel Tapié de Céléyran are visible striding by to the left. But it is the spectral, almost sinister face of a woman who seems to lurch into the scene in the right foreground that dominates the composition. The greenish, masklike visage is that of the dancer May Milton, whom Lautrec depicted much more sympathetically and naturalistically in a painted study for the large canvas.

Stylized, curving surface patterns suggest the influence of Paul Gauguin; but only Lautrec, with his acerbic line, acidic colors, and loose handling, could have conjured so vividly the mixture of disaffection and exhilaration typical of Montmartre's nightlife in this period.

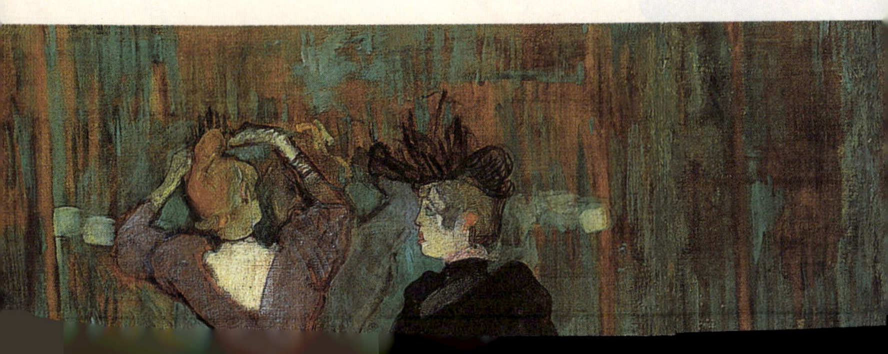

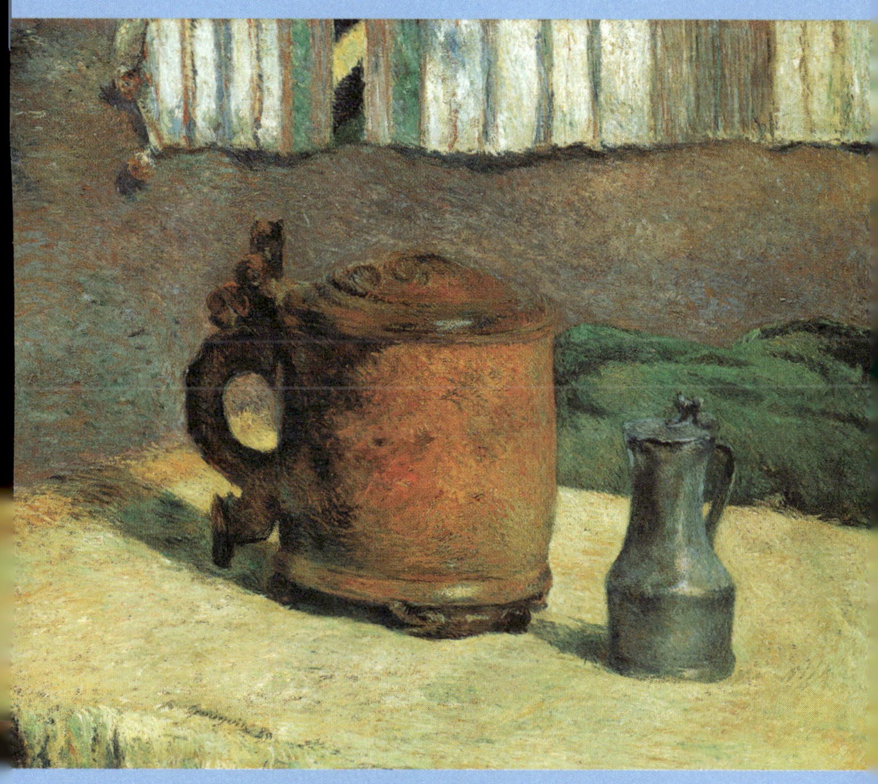

Paul Gauguin (French, 1848–1903), ***Wood Tankard and Metal Jug***, 1880

Paul Gauguin's restless search for a life of "ecstasy, calm, and art" took him on a long, peripatetic journey. He came late to art as a profession; although he had been a collector and amateur painter for many years, he only began to exhibit at the age of twenty-seven, at the fourth Impressionist exhibition, in 1879. Early works such as an 1880 still life of a wooden tankard and pewter jug show his absorption of the blond palette and feathery brushwork of the Impressionists.

During the first of Gauguin's two stays in Tahiti (1891–93), he confronted the fact that the idyllic paradise he had imagined did not exist. Nevertheless, he searched for it in his art. The resulting works—based on the artist's quasi-ethnographic "documents," or drawings of local people and motifs, and on various books, prints, and photographs he had brought with him—are rich amalgams of European and Oceanic forms.

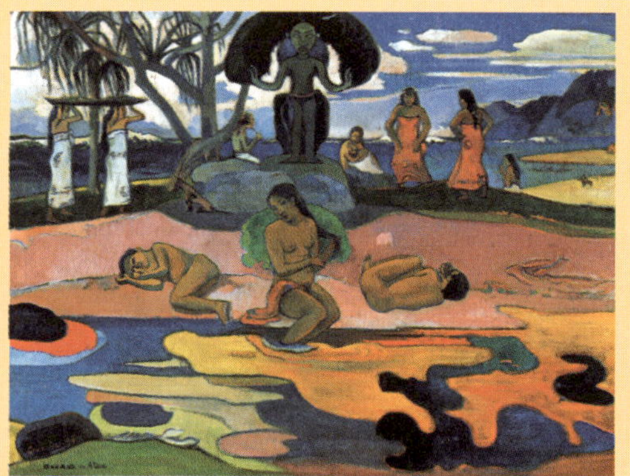

Gauguin, ***Day of the God (Mahana no atua)***, 1894. Gauguin's earlier Tahitian works tend to be more stylized, with sinuous patterns and rich colors taking on lives of their own rather than describing objects.

Gauguin, ***Why Are You Angry? (No te aha oe riri)***, 1896 ▶

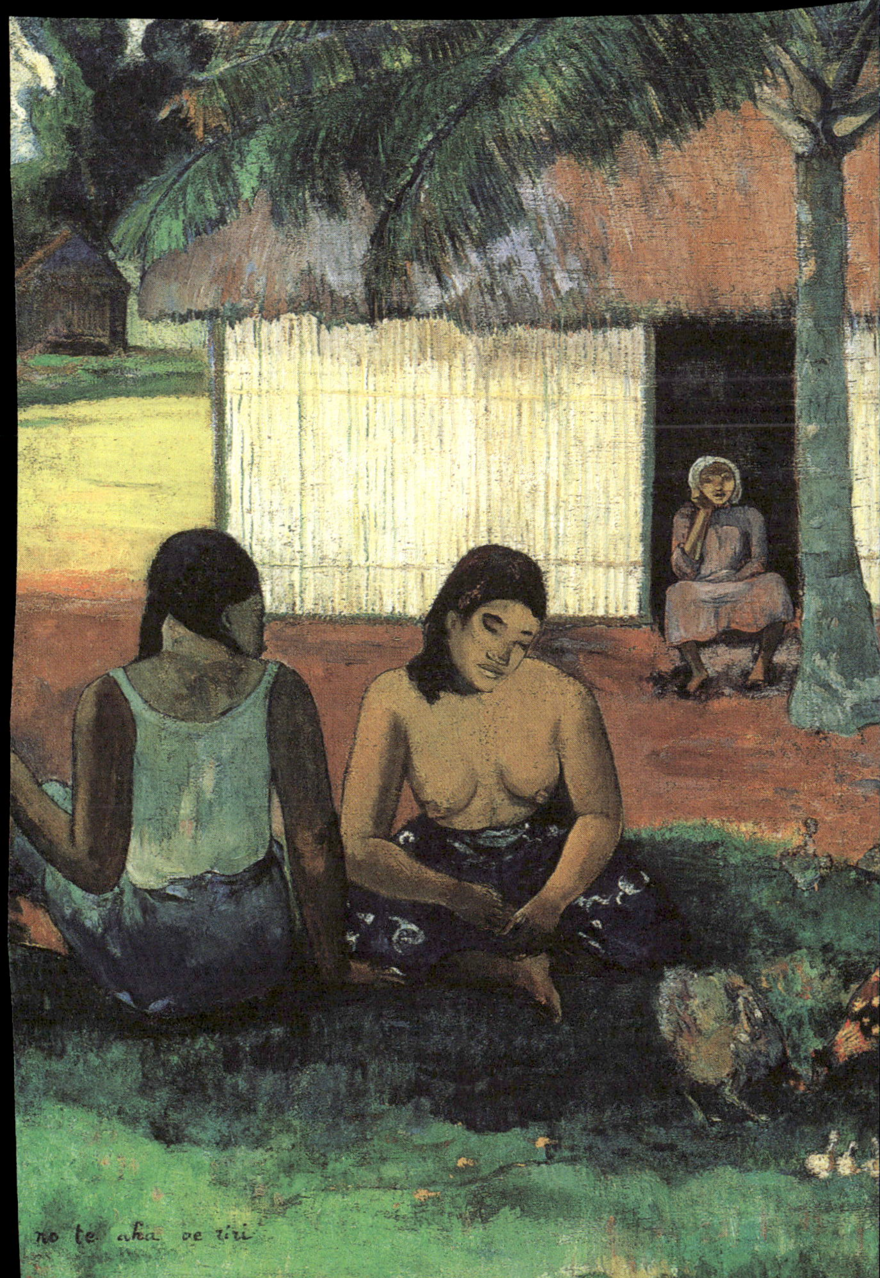
no te aha oe riri

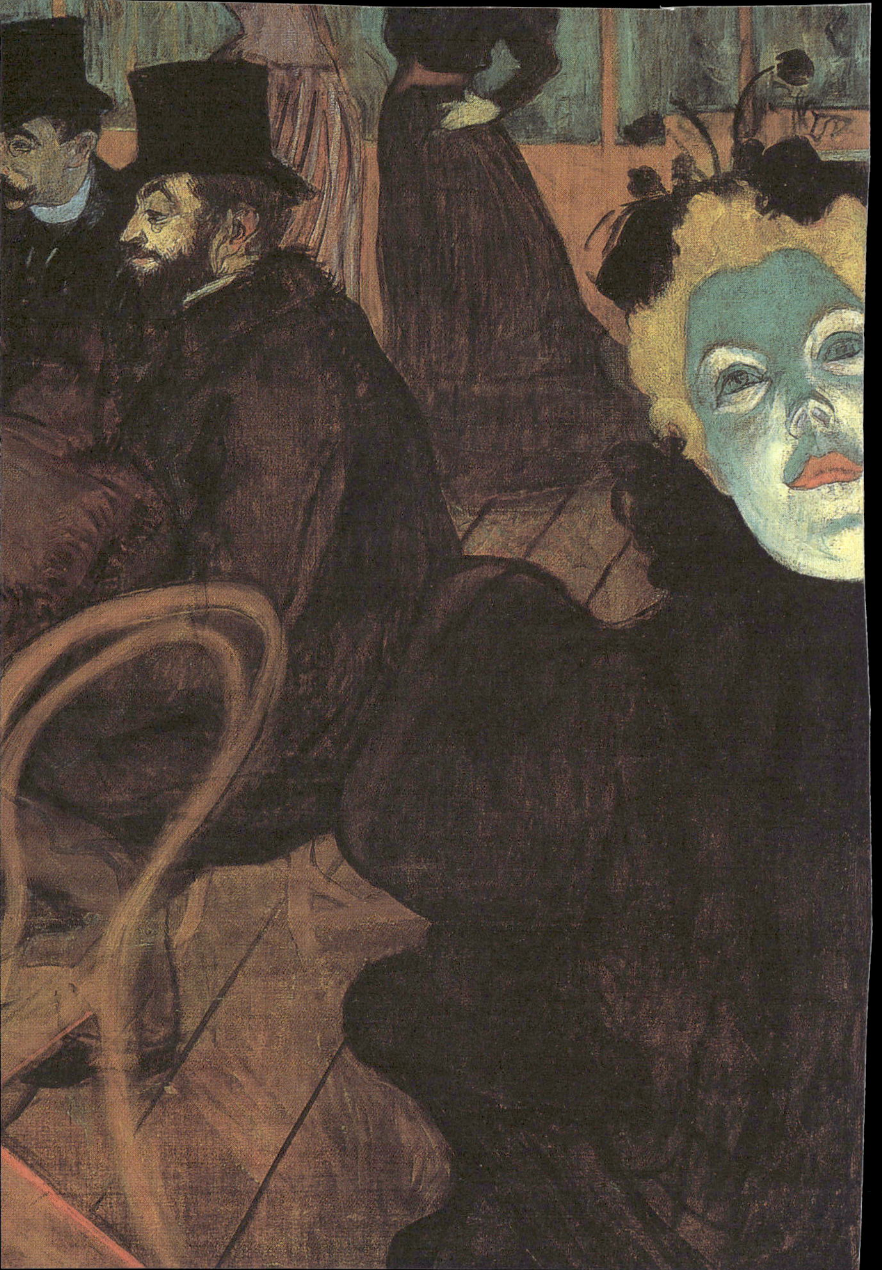

Why Are You Angry? (No te aha oe riri) is one of six large canvases of identical dimensions that Gauguin created during the first months of his second sojourn in Tahiti (1895–1901). Like the other paintings in the group, it exhibits a compositional amplitude and chromatic subtlety new to the artist's work. The interrogative title invites narrative readings, but the composition itself resists definitive interpretation. We are probably meant to associate the question with the pouting, bare-chested woman in the foreground; perhaps it is being posed by her companion. The proximity of two hens and several chicks to the brooding figure, together with the latter's milk-heavy breasts, suggest that recent motherhood is the cause of her discontent. She may be jealous of the woman standing at right, whose elegance and serene self-satisfaction point to a sensual existence unfettered by familial obligations. As in other paintings, Gauguin here cultivated an aura of mystery that prevents any single explanation.

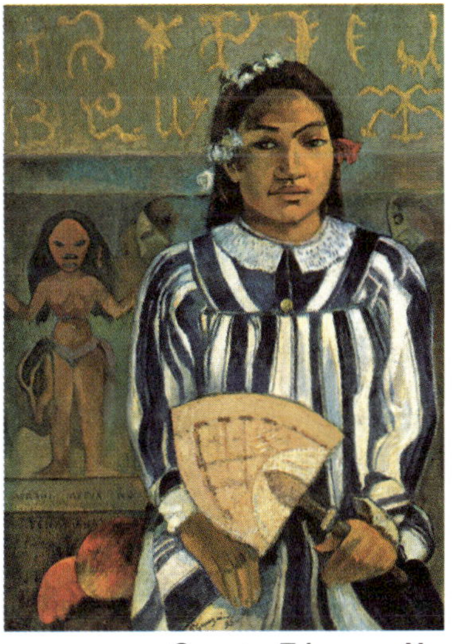

Gauguin, ***Tehamana Has Many Parents (Merahi metua no Tehamana)***, 1893. Gauguin's young Tahitian companion, Tehamana, clothed in a type of dress introduced by western missionaries, is posed here against a background of "native" motifs largely imagined by the artist.

Gauguin soon turned away from the optical-based aesthetic of Impressionism toward greater stylization; he wrote to a fellow artist in 1888: "A piece of advice, do not imitate nature. Art is an abstraction; draw it out from nature while dreaming in front of it and think more about the act of creation than about the result; it is the only way to ascend to God while imitating our divine master in the process of creation."

Gauguin, ***Arlésiennes (Mistral)***, 1888.
Created during the time he spent with Van Gogh in Arles, this work shows Gauguin's experimentation with bold forms and colors to emphasize surface pattern.

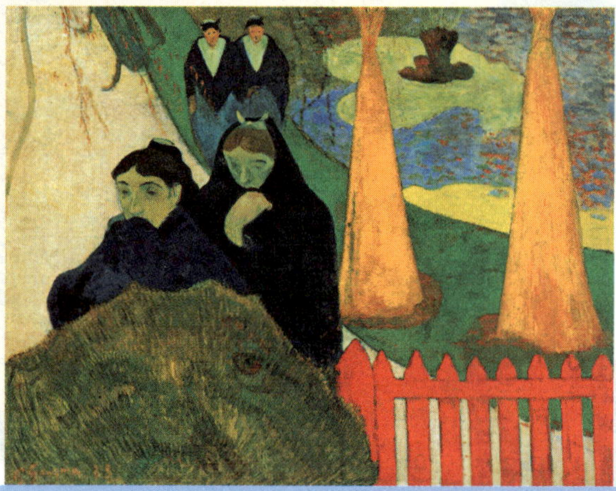

Beginning in the late 1880s, he increasingly favored simplified forms and flat fields of color, allied in his mind with an innocence that had been lost in modern metropolitan culture. The idea that artistic and spiritual truth lay with more "primitive," and thus uncorrupted, cultures led him first to isolated Brittany in northern France and tradition-bound Arles in the south and then to the remote French colonies of Tahiti and the Marquesas islands.

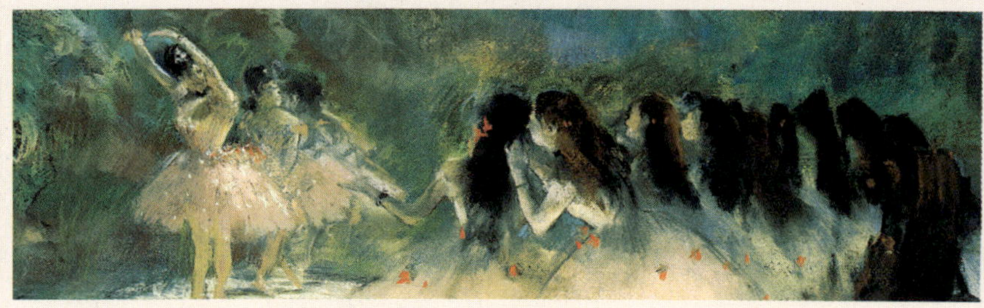

Degas, detail; ***Ballet at the Paris Opéra***, 1876/77

p. 3. Gift of Mr. and Mrs. Gordon Palmer, Mrs. Bertha P. Thorne, Mr. and Mrs. Arthur M. Wood, and Mrs. Rose M. Palmer, 1963.923.

pp. 4–7. *Ballet*: Gift of Mary and Leigh Block, 1981.12; *The Star*: Bequest of Mrs. Diego Suarez, 1980.414.

pp. 8–9. *Woman*: Mr. and Mrs. Martin A. Ryerson Collection, 1937.1025; *Acrobats*: Potter Palmer Collection, 1922.440.

pp. 10–13. *Two Sisters*: Mr. and Mrs. Lewis Larned Coburn Memorial Collection; *Lunch at the Restaurant Fournaise*: Potter Palmer Collection, 1922.437.

p. 15. Restricted gift of Susan and Lewis Manilow, 1991.28.

pp. 16–19. Charles H. and Mary F. S. Worcester Collection, 1964.336.

pp. 20–21. Mr. and Mrs. Martin A. Ryerson Collection, 1933.1158.

pp. 22–25. *Autumn*: Mr. and Mrs. Lewis Larned Coburn Memorial Collection, 1933.444; *Thaw, Sunset*: Gift of Mr. and Mrs. Daniel C. Searle, 1983.166; *Snow Effect, Overcast Day*: Mr. and Mrs. Martin A. Ryerson Collection, 1933.1155; *Sunset, Snow Effect*: Potter Palmer Collection, 1922.431; *Stack of Wheat*: Restricted gift of the Searle Family Trust; Major Acquisitions Centennial Endowment; through prior acquisitions of the Mr. and Mrs. Martin A. Ryerson and Potter Palmer Collections; through prior bequest of Jerome Friedman, 1983.29; *End of Summer*: Gift of Arthur M. Wood in memory of Pauline Palmer Wood, 1985.1103.

pp. 26–27. *Seated Woman*: Bequest of Abby Aldrich Rockefeller, 1999.7v; *Trees*: Helen Regenstein Collection, 1966.184.

pp. 28–31. Helen Birch Bartlett Memorial Collection, 1926.224.

pp. 32–33. Joseph Winterbotham Collection, 1954.326.

pp. 34–37. *Bedroom*: Helen Birch Bartlett Memorial Collection, 1926.417; *Madame Roulin*: Helen Birch Bartlett Memorial Collection, 1926.200; *Poet's Garden*: Mr. and Mrs. Lewis Larned Coburn Memorial Collection, 1933.433.

pp. 38–39. Mr. and Mrs. Carter H. Harrison Collection, 1954.1193.

pp. 40–43. *Moulin Rouge*: Helen Birch Bartlett Memorial Collection, 1928.610; *May Milton*: Bequest of Kate L. Brewster, 1949.263.

pp. 44–45. *Wood Tankard*: Millennium Gift of Sarah Lee Corporation, 1999.362; *Arlésiennes*: Mr. and Mrs. Lewis Larned Coburn Memorial Collection, 1934.391.

pp. 46–49. *Why Are You Angry?*: Mr. and Mrs. Martin A. Ryerson Collection, 1933.1119; *Day of the God*: Helen Birch Bartlett Memorial Collection, 1926.198; *Tehamana*: Gift of Mr. and Mrs. Charles Deering McCormick, 1980.613,

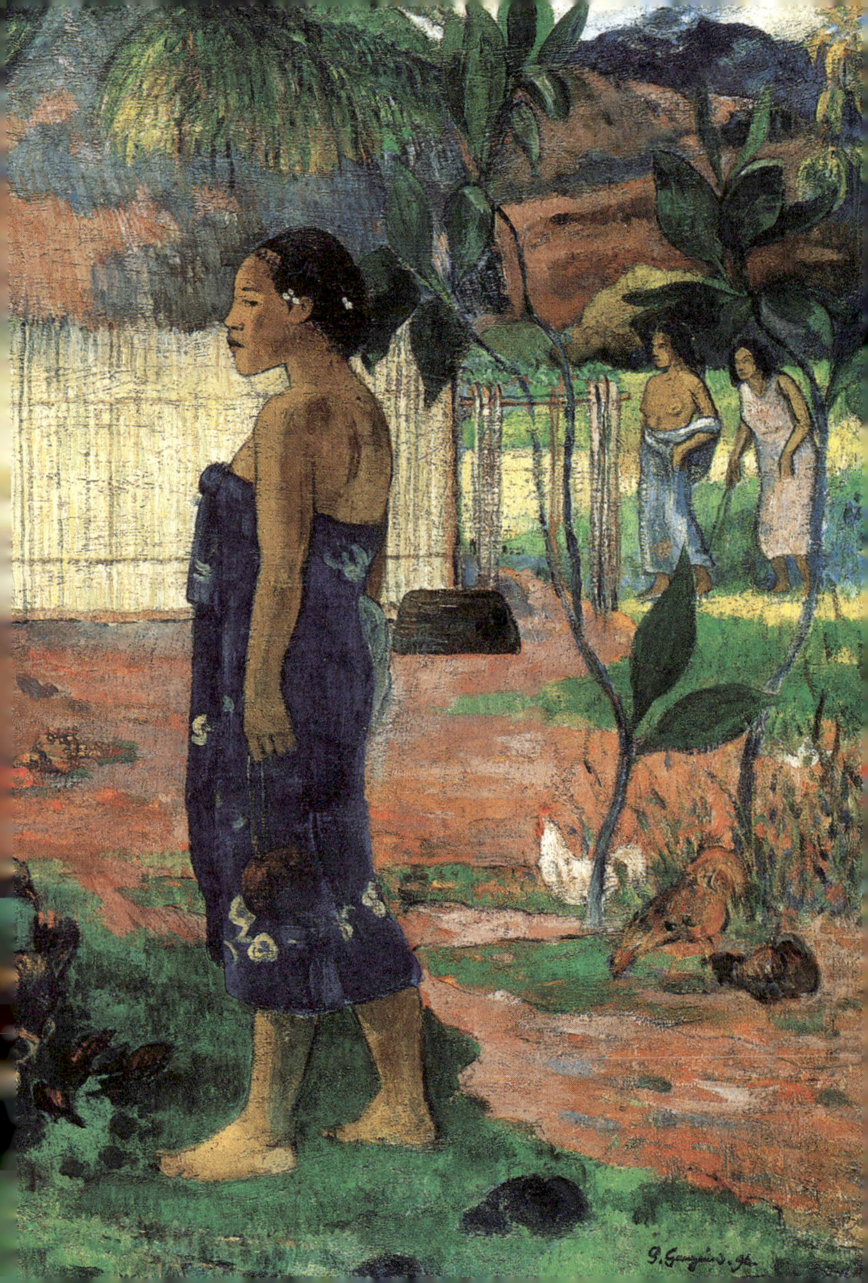
P. Gauguin. 94